Alan Hargrave was born in Leeds and trained as an engineer before working for ten years with the Anglican Church in South America, first in economic development in Argentina, then church planting in Bolivia. He returned to the UK in 1987 to train as a priest. After eleven years as vicar of a council estate parish in Cambridge, he became Canon Missioner of Ely Cathedral in 2004. *An Almighty Passion: Meeting God in ordinary life* was published in 2002 (reissued in 2011) and *Living Well: Finding a rule of life to sustain & revitalize us* in 2010. Alan entered the 'Jubilee Years' of retirement in January 2016. He remains passionate about justice, Yorkshire cricket, golf, his four children – one of whom tragically died of cancer – his grandchildren, his wife Annie and, of course, the Almighty.

Magpie

One for sorrow
Two for joy
Three for a girl and four for a boy
Five for silver
Six for gold
Seven for a secret never to be told.

one
for
sorrow

A memoir of death and life

ALAN HARGRAVE

First published in Great Britain in 2017

Society for Promoting Christian Knowledge
36 Causton Street
London SW1P 4ST
www.spck.org.uk

British Library Cataloguing-in-Publication Data
A catalogue record for this book is available from the British Library

ISBN 978–0–281–07819–6
eBook ISBN 978–0–281–07820–2

Typeset by Manila Typesetting Company

First printed in Great Britain by Ashford Colour Press
Subsequently digitally printed in Great Britain

eBook by Manila Typesetting Company

Produced on paper from sustainable forests

In memory of Tom, my beloved son

For Annie, Liz, Jo, Ben, Shirley and all who
have walked this journey with us

For all who bear the deep wounds of loss and grief,
especially those who face sorrow much greater than our own

The Well of Grief

Those who will not slip beneath
   the still surface of the well of grief,

turning down through its black water
   to the place we cannot breathe,

will never know the source from which we drink,
   the secret water, cold and clear,

nor find in the darkness glimmering,
   the small round coins,
      thrown away by those who wished for something else.[1]

Contents

Preface: Santa Cruz Bolivia, 1985

Jo Farrington arrives with her four boys in the minibus. She has also brought along our friend, Anjy, and her two girls. Annie calls our children, picks up the packed lunch and they set off for a day at the zoo. Santa Cruz Zoo is definitely worth a visit. Scarlet macaws, three-toed sloths, jaguars, tapirs, capybaras and some very entertaining monkeys – all animals found in Bolivia. The kids love it and they enjoy a great day out. Then it is time to go. The three mums round up the ten children and make for the exit. They climb back into Jo's minibus and head for home, a half-hour drive away. Jo drops off Annie and our children. I make a drink and call everyone into the kitchen. Tom doesn't come. We call him again but he still doesn't come. So, feeling a bit annoyed, we go and look for him: in his room, around the house, in the garden, but he isn't there. He must have gone home with the Farringtons. We ring them, but he isn't there either. They come over to help with the search. We look round the streets, but he's nowhere to be seen. I am trying to keep calm but by now my heart is pounding and my stomach churning. It is hard not to fear the worst. We get everyone together and go through what happened when they left the zoo. They are all adamant that Tom *did* get into the minibus. They remember whom he sat next to and what he said on the way home.

Nevertheless, I decide to go back to the zoo. It is our last chance. I get in the car with our eldest daughter, Liz, and we race round the ring road at a speed I would not normally countenance, hoping there are no police cars, which, luckily, there aren't. We pull up with a screech of brakes outside the zoo. And there, standing patiently outside the zoo, is an old man. In his arms a distraught child, face covered in tears and snot. The man saw the minibus leave, saw Tom left behind, realized what had happened and decided to look after Tom until we returned, which he was sure we would do. He has been waiting patiently, trying to soothe and reassure Tom, for over an hour. We thank the man profusely. We are pathetically grateful. There are more tears. This time tears of relief. Liz takes Tom in her arms and sits with him on her knee. I drive back, a lot more slowly and carefully than I drove there.

Memory is a strange thing. It plays tricks on us. We forget things that happened. We remember things that didn't. And sometimes we give very different accounts of the same thing which we all experienced. As I write down my memories of Tom's illness and death, and its lasting impact upon us, I am all too aware that these are *my* memories. Memories often sharp and painful – perhaps too painful to remember in some cases. Memories confused and reworked in the ten plus years since Tom died. I am sure that if Annie, one of our other children, or someone else close to us through that time, were to write their memories, they would be overlapping, but very different.

So this is my story of Tom's illness, his death and of, in particular, my struggle to live through it. I thought when I started that I was writing about Tom, but I realize now that it is largely about me. About how I, as someone in the public eye, as a vicar, dealt, and failed to deal, with my son's death.

It is not always in chronological order, since some events would otherwise have spanned several chapters and lost their meaning. Some people's names have been changed to protect their identity. It is also incomplete. It is not possible or necessary to include everything. And some things are too personal to include. Nevertheless, it is a very personal account. I share it because others have encouraged me to write it down. I share it because I have read too many sanitized accounts of death that simply do not ring true. I share it because I know that we are not the only ones to face such pain and loss. Indeed, many people face pain and loss which is utterly catastrophic, which destroys their lives. I share it hoping that, through these pages, my story might resonate with some of the painful stories each of us bears inside. That through it, others might find some key to help unlock their own grief. After all, as the Turkish proverb says:

Those who cannot express their grief find no remedy for it.

Finally, this comes with an apology. A common symptom of grief is anger. I have seen this a hundred times in the people I meet in the course of my ministry. People who do not recognize anger as a normal part of grief and thus let rip on some poor, unfortunate person who becomes the focus of their anger. Yet, despite knowing all this, I realize now, looking back, that it is exactly what I did, too. Thinking my anger was righteous, justified, when in fact it was just my inability to cope, my being overwhelmed by grief and pain, all my defences down, shattered, unable to take any more. And maybe it was, too, my misplaced anger at God, who wasn't tangible enough to shout at in any satisfactory way. So to all those of you who had to cope with my anger and bear the sharp edge of my tongue, I am truly sorry.

Acknowledgements

I am more grateful than I can say to Annie, Liz, Jo and Ben for correcting my flawed memories and adding important events which I had neglected to mention. I am particularly grateful to them for allowing this very personal account to be written and made public, but most of all, I am deeply thankful for each one of them, for they have loved me even when I was unlovable and beyond reach.

I am grateful, too, to all who have stood by us, and by Tom. Some of you appear in the text but many of you do not. Without you we could not have lived through it. Thank you.

Not just for their professional skill, but for being deeply caring human beings, we will be forever grateful to those who looked after Tom through the East Barnwell Health Centre and at Addenbrooke's Hospital, in particular Stephen Barclay, Tom's GP, and Pippa Corrie, his consultant oncologist.

Thank you to the people of Christ the Redeemer, especially my colleague Ank, who held the fort and held me up when I could no longer stand upright. And more recently thank you to my cathedral colleagues who carried the extra load in the study leave during which I wrote this book. Also to Ro, Archie and others at the mooring who gave me space, electricity and cups of coffee while I sat on our narrowboat, writing.

1

Unwell

It's a normal day in late May. Tom goes off on his bike, as usual, to Sainsbury's, where he works in the bakery. That night he arrives home with a bad headache. He takes a couple of paracetamol and thinks no more of it, but the following morning it is still there. He takes some more pills and sets off for work. He gets back later that day and it is worse. What's more, he is beginning to suffer from double vision. More paracetamol. Annie and I don't like the look of it and suggest he give work a miss and go to the doctor, but Tom is far too conscientious for that and doesn't want to let anyone down. By the end of the following day he is really struggling. He not only has a severe headache, barely made tolerable by the painkillers, but the double vision has turned into a definite squint. We plead with him to see the doctor but he assures us he will be OK. However, he has a terrible night and the following morning, a Saturday, we finally persuade him to go to the emergency surgery. We run him there in the car and at 9 a.m. we are called in to see the doctor.

As luck would have it, it turns out to be our own GP on duty. He examines Tom carefully, expresses some concern and then rings up and makes an appointment with the Neurology Department at Addenbrooke's Hospital. We drive straight to Addenbrooke's. We do not know it yet, but it is a journey we will repeat endlessly over the coming weeks. By 11 a.m. he is being examined by the Neurology Registrar. He thinks it may just be a severe migraine and gives Tom some stronger painkillers. If it doesn't clear up we are to return the following week.

Annie has a work trip booked to Colombia for a few days. Tom's illness doesn't look serious so off she goes. However, the symptoms do not clear up. They get worse, a lot worse. On top of the severe headaches and double vision Tom starts to vomit. He cannot keep anything down. Eventually he is admitted to hospital, to the neurology ward. They try their best but they cannot control the symptoms. He cannot even keep down the anti-emetics, which are supposed to stop the vomiting.

When he was a baby, in La Paz, Bolivia, Tom contracted salmonella. Whether it was the result of the salmonella itself or the treatment which followed we do not know, but ever since then, whenever he is ill, he always suffers this vomiting reaction. Once it starts he cannot take anything orally, not even water. In South America it was not such a problem, because a lot of drugs are available as anal suppositories and to 'colocar un suero' ('put up a drip') was seen as a very normal practice. Indeed, people feeling a bit off colour would often go to the local chemist or nursing station and have them set up a dextrose drip, which, temporarily at least, made them feel better. Countries have very different attitudes to the administration of drugs. In France, you often get an injection. In Germany, suppositories are freely available. In England we seem to be keen on taking drugs orally, if at all possible.

We explain to the doctors about Tom's vomiting reaction and suggest they give him drugs by suppository, injection or drip. They listen, but they do not seem to take on board what we are saying. So they only use injections or a drip when he is in serious danger of becoming dehydrated. Then it's back to the pills. After a while he starts vomiting again. They give him pills to stop the vomiting, which he immediately vomits up. We beg them to set up a drip or give him an anti-emetic injection, but to no avail. They are decent, caring people, doing their best for Tom, carrying out all the tests under the sun, but they have their way of doing things. On this issue, they fail to listen to us, though it is not for want of our repeating the message: 'Once he starts vomiting he cannot take anything orally. Honestly. We know. We have been here before. Often.'

Tom is no stranger to illness, even from birth – maybe even before birth. His is a difficult pregnancy and Annie is ill for a good part of it. Then there is a lot of false labour. When, finally, he is born (in Leeds, while we are home on leave from South America) he fails to breathe for some time. I wonder, later, if this is the start of all his problems? Then he has a very bad reaction to a measles jab. When he is six months old, we return to South America, to work in La Paz, Bolivia. Almost immediately he contracts salmonella and is very seriously ill, in hospital for many days, on a drip, unable to keep anything down. He recovers from the infection but his digestive system has been permanently damaged. Diarrhoea and vomiting become normal. He doesn't absorb his food properly. Despite our best efforts, he 'fails to thrive'.

A couple of years later we go on holiday to the Yungas, a semi-tropical area, down a dangerous mountain pass, away from the altitude of La Paz, where we live at 12,000 feet above sea level. While we are there Tom is as well as he'd ever been, but on the long, vertiginous road back up the mountain, he turns pale and begins to vomit again. Whatever problems he has are clearly exacerbated by altitude. We need to leave La Paz.

We leave La Paz and head back to England, on leave. Endless tests at Birmingham Children's Hospital find nothing wrong, so the following spring we return to Bolivia, to Santa Cruz this time, in the lowlands. That's when the tonsillitis starts. Despite almost continuous antibiotics he has tonsillitis at least once a month. As always, once he becomes ill, the vomiting reaction kicks in.

So life is a struggle for Tom. He struggles to grow – he is always shorter than his mates and, particularly annoying for him, shorter than his younger brother. He struggles academically, which is not picked up, because he is well behaved and not at all disruptive. He just sits quietly at the back and fails to flourish: a typical, middle-class low-flyer.

So Tom is no stranger to ill health. He lies on his hospital bed, continuing to suffer, silently, stoically, doubled up with pain and retching to bring up the last remnants of an already empty stomach. There are endless tests and scans. Endless questions – sometimes intrusive, personal questions – repeating the same information to yet another set of doctors. There are ridiculous questions: 'Do you regularly inspect your son's body for moles?' I mean, for God's sake, he is 21!

He has been in hospital for several weeks. It is clear that, whatever the problem is, it is serious. The doctors are keen to get him home while they await the results of yet more tests. His symptoms are reasonably controlled and he is not vomiting at the moment. They give us painkillers and anti-emetics to take home. We ask if they can supply them as suppositories but, apparently, they can't. His sisters, Liz and Jo, have come home from Nottingham and Sheffield. His younger brother, Ben, is still at home. So there are several of us to look after him. Liz is a nurse, which is to prove invaluable in the coming months. However, coming home, for Tom, is not a success. After a couple of days he starts vomiting again. The oral medication is useless. We take him back to Addenbrooke's. Unfortunately he cannot be admitted straight back on to the neurology ward, so he is kept in A & E for hours, on a trolley, desperately ill. It is an experience neither he, nor we, are keen to repeat.

2

Fire

As I said at the beginning, these are my memories. Others remember things differently. Remember things I have forgotten or buried. Here is one of Annie's memories.

Where is the chapter on the fire?!

When Alan showed me the first draft of the book I couldn't believe the fire wasn't there! I remind him about what happened – 'Oh, yes . . . we did . . . it was . . . I'd forgotten . . .' – but it has been lost from his mind, beneath the clamour of other memories crying out for inclusion.

So he asks me to write about the fire. I agree because, although so many of our memories from that time are individual – we were so emotionally divorced from each other in the struggle to get through each day – this one was certainly shared. For me, as the main carrier of this memory, it shouts out loud. I couldn't consent to the manuscript being sent off to the publisher without including it.

It is still early on in Tom's illness – 'BD'. 'Before Diagnosis.' A time before loss bit so savagely deep. Though we were already on the road. The Barnwell Road, where we only ever saw one solitary magpie.

It is the weekend of the Queen's Golden Jubilee. The sun is shining. I am just back from two weeks working in Colombia and I have a couple of days' leave, in addition to the bank holiday. The plan is to go down to the narrowboat we keep on the River Cam, to do what we always do there – sleep long hours, eat, drink, walk, catch up with each other, make love, leave the demands of work and world behind and rediscover why we married each other in the first place.

Tom is in hospital, very poorly. I have no heart for the boat, but I have been away, a long way away. Alan has been here, in and out of hospital, living with the strain, the fear, trying to keep up with his work. He very much needs to go. So we go, for just two days, staying just one night away from home, while other family members accompany Tom.

We moor up on the left bank of the Cam, north of Cambridge, by a small grassy bank. A delightful place which we know of old. A well-used fishing ground and a place for boats to stop and stay. It is surrounded by trees and lush summer growth, with the towpath up a short slope, should you want to walk. A pleasant, lazy place in the middle of summer.

But, oh! The big tree, whose shade we have often enjoyed, has gone. The discarded branches are strewn around. We can clearly see the ravages of disease in the stump. It is still the place we know, but now changed for ever. The beautiful tree cut down. Felled beyond returning. No going back to the settled, familiar place it had been. No undoing the injury.

We stand for a while. I don't remember how long. We roam over the ground, sighing, taking it in. In the centre, near the stump, are the remains of a small, recent fireplace, a black patch amid the green, drawing our eyes to it.

Did we say anything to each other? Exchange words? Did we make a plan? Decide what to do?

Slowly, gradually, we gather dry twigs and branches and build a fire. Somehow it is lit. A crackle of flames springs up, eating the old wood. A good fire on a dry day, with little smoke. Soon a roaring blaze.

This fire is not for cooking. In any case, I am indifferent to food, already in a tunnel of eating as a chore, the sour tastes and spiny textures to be chewed and swallowed down because I have to. A steamy portion of mashed potato giving no comfort or pleasure now. A lush, red plum no longer an invitation to a riot of juices to enjoy. This is no nourishing fire. Rather a consuming fire. Demanding of us to feed its devouring appetite. Which we do.

We stand watching it. Just watching and feeding it. There is no conversation, no reflecting on the past weeks, no laughter, no dreaming of the future. This is no comfortable, convivial fire.

We gather more and more branches. Each time the fire burns down we silently replenish it, feeding its hunger. The flames hold us mesmerized. We keep on burning. Burning. Burning. I do not know how long we stay there. An hour? Two? Maybe eternity.

I don't ask what it means but we catch its power. I don't know what it signifies, but we cannot stop. Compelled to burn. To watch. To burn. Especially to burn. There is no memory of leaving that place or when we cruised away.

The shadow of death is not yet articulated. No concrete questions: 'What are we facing?' 'How long?' It isn't their time, yet. These questions are still in the queue, awaiting our arrival.

The curtain of flame deflects us from our worst fears. Not yet. Not yet. We are still BD. BD. Not yet the funeral pyre.

For now, just a fire.

3

Bad news

———•◦•———

Tom's discovery of a lump under his right arm confirms in our minds what we fear most. This has to be cancer. A little knowledge is a dangerous thing. Like most people these days, we scour the internet. Based on his symptoms and age, we think he may have Hodgkin's lymphoma. Not good, but treatable with radio- and chemotherapy – and with a five-year survival rate of over 80 per cent. We brace ourselves for the battle ahead but are cautiously optimistic about the future.

With Tom, we meet Mr Grant, the surgeon who is to remove the lump from under Tom's arm and do a biopsy. He is efficient and reassuring and a few days later the lump is removed. Then the waiting. Why does it take so long? Surely it's just about looking at it under the microscope, isn't it? They suggest it will be about ten days; but ten days come and go.

I am booked in for our annual clergy golf tournament at Frilford Heath, near Oxford, in a couple of days' time. Two rounds of golf on a tough course with a slap-up lunch and tea to follow. Exhausting, but a grand day out. At least it will take my mind off things for a while. I plan to be away with my mates overnight. With an early start and an 8 p.m. finish, it is too much to drive there and back in a day. I wonder about cancelling it but, when we enquire at the hospital, they seem to think the results will still take another few days, so off we set.

The journey there is all blokeish hilarity, particularly on the subject of Michael's white-knuckle driving and Bruce's unwillingness to pay more than a fiver for his dinner at the pub that evening – not to mention his unwillingness to split the bill four ways when he's had sausage and mash and we've all had the rack of lamb and a dessert. We've booked in at a B & B for the night, just a mile from the course. We get back to the B & B from the pub at about 11 p.m. and go to bed.

There is a message on my bed from the B & B owners: 'Please phone home urgently.' The phone has now taken on a different significance. It is no longer the bearer of loving greetings from Annie or the kids, or even the neutral conveyor of details about work; it is the bringer of bad tidings. I ring home. As I wait for Annie to pick up the phone, I feel the tension in my body. She tells me that she has tried to ring me earlier, on my mobile, but for some reason hasn't got through. I hear her voice and know from the tone that all is not well. The results are in. They confirm our worst fears. Tom does indeed have cancer. There are no more details yet, but there is an appointment at the hospital, 11 a.m. tomorrow, to talk to the oncologist. 'Will you come back?' 'Of course I will.'

However, there are no trains that will get me to Cambridge tonight and we've all had a drink, so I am not happy to accept Michael's generous offer to drive me home immediately. Michael is keen to take me in the car the following morning, but I do not want to ruin everyone else's golf and, in any case, something inside me wants to be alone. So we arrange for him to drop me at Didcot station at 6 a.m. Annie picks me up from Cambridge station and by 11 a.m. we are at Tom's bedside, waiting for the oncologist.

Some years ago I attended a seminar for clergy on 'breaking bad news'. It was led by an expert in palliative care. He said he thought that there were two extremes of doctors – those who are determined to tell you the stark truth and those who avoid it at any cost. And also two extremes of patients/relatives – those who want to know the worst and those who don't. I think I am definitely towards the 'wanting to know the worst' end of the scale. However, Dr Roberts, the oncology registrar, is clearly seeking to soften the blow.

Tom is in a side ward now, so at least we will have some privacy. Dr Roberts is very kind but also clearly nervous. He also has a slight stutter, made worse, no doubt, by the gravity of the occasion. He gently explains to us that Tom has malignant melanoma. 'Isn't that skin cancer? How come they never found a mole on his skin? Can't it be treated with laser surgery?' Dr Roberts explains that no primary site has been found, which is very unusual. They have removed the tumour from under his arm, but there is one growing on the optic nerve, which is what is causing so much pain and double vision. He tells us that they will arrange a course of radiotherapy which they hope will alleviate the pain in his head.

'What about chemotherapy? When will that start?' I ask. He looks grave as he hesitantly explains that there are no known chemotherapy agents which are effective against this type of cancer. 'What are you planning to do then? What is the treatment? What is the prognosis?' Dr Roberts is very nervous indeed now and his stutter has got worse. He talks about a possible period of remission. Finally, he says:
'The thththththththththhing is
iiiiiiiiiiiiit's
iiiiiiiincurable.'

It is like a tidal wave hitting us. Hitting Tom. This 21-year-old with everything to live for, full of hopes and dreams. Making plans to trek round Australia with his best mate, Phil. The hopes and dreams are all, now, suddenly shattered. Incurable. We are utterly stunned.

I am about to question Dr Roberts further, but Annie gives me the look which says: 'We can't take any more just now. Leave it.' So, unlike me, I do.

Dr Roberts leaves. Tom is very quiet. He curls up in the foetal position and turns his face to the wall. He doesn't want to speak. Indeed, there are no words. He cannot speak. Neither can we.

The rest of us eventually head home in silence. We get out of the car, walk into the downstairs back room and weep, crying out in deep, uncontrollable gasps of grief: 'Poor Tom. Poor Tom. Poor Tom.'

4

Loss

———————

As the terrible diagnosis starts to sink in, we begin instead to think about remission. Perhaps Tom will buck all the trends and have three or four years, instead of the more likely three or four months. With the lump under his arm removed and after he has had radiotherapy, surely there will be a decent period of good health? At least we will have some quality time together, won't we?

So, based on an over-optimistic view of what the medics are telling us, we decide to book a holiday. Crete: somewhere warm and welcoming, in autumn, when Tom is feeling better. We can all go, as a family, and enjoy each other, one last time. Of course, it is not possible to get insurance for Tom because of his diagnosis, but we've been given some money for a holiday and we decide to take the risk. We go into Lunn Poly and Andrea books it all up for us. A package holiday, in a villa with the privacy of our own pool. Ideal. At least we have something to look forward to. Remission. We cannot bear to think about the long term, but we can live now, for a while at least, despite the knot of fear which constantly punches us, deep in our guts.

Day by day we drive up Barnwell Road, Perne Road, Mowbray Road to the hospital. On the Barnwell Road, between two housing estates, there is a stretch of trees, bordering on Coldham's Common. As I drive past, a solitary magpie flies up into the trees. That well-known rhyme, signature tune of an old children's TV programme, springs into my mind: 'One for sorrow'. I try to dismiss it from my thoughts. I don't think of myself as superstitious or prone to seeing signs. Also, magpies are pretty

11

solitary birds, so it is normal to see just one on its own. All the same, I cannot help myself. On the way home there it is again. A solitary magpie, harbinger of death. 'One for sorrow,' it squawks, as it flies up into the trees. Almost every time I pass, day after day, going and coming back, it's there. Just the one. I drive past again. There it is. 'One for sorrow' hammering home what is already lodged deep within me.

Waiting with Hagar

On the Barnwell Road
At the edge,
On the grass,
On the Common side,
Once there were four.
Just once.
 'Four for a boy.'
But apart from that
Each time
Going or coming
It's always one.
 'One for sorrow.'
Day after day
 'One for sorrow'
Another scan
 'One for sorrow'
The foetal curl
 'One for sorrow'
The bowl of vomit
 'One for sorrow'
The telltale lump
 'One for sorrow'
The death-ray mask
 'One for sorrow'
The surgeon's knife
 'One for sorrow'

The knot of fear in the pit of my stomach
    'One for sorrow'
'I cannot bear to sit and watch my son die.'[1]
    Magpie.

People talk about the heart as the focus of emotion. For me, however, it is the stomach, the guts: churning, tight and tense. I am, at least, in good company. In the Gospels, when it says that Jesus was 'deeply moved', it often literally means: 'He felt it in his bowels.' Not much comfort, but at least he gets it. Does it help to think that God knows how I feel? That he has been there? Got the T-shirt? Frankly, it doesn't, just now, but maybe one day it will. Another trip to the hospital and there it is again. The solitary magpie. 'One for sorrow.' My stomach churns again and I brace myself for more bad news.

Tom is a great sports fan and the World Cup is taking place, but he is too ill even to watch the England matches on the TV monitor by his bed. Stephen, our excellent GP, has found out what is happening and has got involved. His immediate reaction is: 'We must get Tom home.' Hospital is certainly not the place you want to be when you are dying, but after our earlier, failed attempt to get him home we, and especially Tom, are very wary. What we had not realized, however, is that, as well as being our GP, Stephen is a Macmillan Research Fellow in palliative care. It turns out he is an expert on pain relief and symptom control. Within a week Tom is home, with a syringe driver and all the drugs he needs, which Liz can administer if necessary. We have Stephen's emergency mobile number should we need it and an agreement that Tom can be admitted straight back to the ward, not via A & E, if necessary. The pain and nausea are never completely absent, but they are at least under better control. Things are beginning to look more hopeful.

A cast of Tom's head is taken and a plastic mask is made to hold his head still while they perform the radiotherapy. It looks like a death mask. It is. There are still regular trips up the

Barnwell Road – outpatient appointments with the oncologist; radiotherapy appointments; appointments with the eye specialist; follow-up with the surgeon; more scans.

Our optimism is short-lived. His eye does not get better and he needs to wear a patch over it to avoid the double vision. The doctor explains to us that the melanoma produces 'seedlings' which are carried around the body, in the bloodstream, and can grow anywhere. It all sounds so innocuous. 'Seedlings.' Such a friendly word. One we associate with gardening, with springtime, with growth and new life. These seedlings, though, are floating around Tom's body like hungry wolves, looking for a tasty morsel of liver, kidney, lung, nerve or brain to land on and devour. They, too, are harbingers of death. They are eating my son alive.

We are regular visitors to the oncology department. Walking up its long tunnel of a corridor. Sitting in the waiting room. Looking at other people with the same yellow, swollen, steroid features and no hair. Wondering what awaits them. Annie and I are sitting one day, waiting. Always waiting. Tom is seeing the consultant. After a while Annie turns to me and squeezes my hand. 'It's our wedding anniversary,' she says. I have completely forgotten.

Our sense of loss is great, but we are not the worst off, by any means. Annie and I go off for a couple of days' break again on our narrowboat, cruising just a few miles up the river and mooring at Wicken Fen for the night. It is almost dark when someone bangs on the boat door. It is a remote spot and we are not expecting anyone else to be around. Warily, I answer the door. It is a small group of men. They ask us if we have seen two young girls. They explain that they have disappeared from the village just up the road and that they are one of the many search parties out looking for them. The village is Soham. The girls are Holly and Jessica, whose murdered bodies will be found in the woods a few days later. Death is not the worst thing that can happen to you. There is always someone worse off than you. In this case, much worse.

Tom begins to have trouble speaking. At first we think it is just a sore throat, but it doesn't go away. It is another tumour, growing on the vocal chords. We see Dr Corrie, his consultant oncologist, for the results of the latest scan. It reveals that there are now about 20 tumours developing, in glands in his chest and abdomen. She tells us, sadly, that there is nothing they can do about them. Tom and I walk slowly back down the long oncology corridor, towards the car park. Walking together in silence. Eventually, in a croaky voice, Tom whispers to me: 'It looks rather bleak.' I can think of nothing at all to say in reply.

'Rather bleak' is a complete understatement. Tom is not just suffering from the cancer now but also the side effects of the drugs. He is swollen and bloated with the high doses of steroids. The painkillers cause terrible constipation and, although it is controlled to some extent, he is never free from pain and nausea. His energy levels are falling, day by day. Some of the tumours begin to be visible, under the skin. It is relentless. There is no stopping it and there is to be no remission. It is loss upon loss. Loss upon loss. This is only going one way, and much, much faster than we had hoped, prayed or expected.

Early on, when he was first admitted to hospital, we bought him a balloon, which we tied to the end of his hospital bed. After the diagnosis, I bring it home. On it are the now hollow words: 'Get Well Soon'. It is crumpled and beginning to deflate. I cannot bear to look at it any more. I take it into the garden and let it go, then stand and watch its painfully slow progress, rising above the garden, above the house, above the trees. I strain to follow it with my eyes, afraid of losing sight of it. A tiny dot in the sky. Then it is gone and I know in my heart that, soon, Tom will be gone as well.

5

Bottom line – 1

One of the problems of being the vicar is that you are a public figure. There is no retreating quietly into your own struggles and grief. Everyone is watching you. Everyone knows. More so in a parish like this, a council estate where people do not generally have a lot of confidence in themselves. They look to the vicar for faith and spiritual strength: 'Hi, Alan. Say one for me!' But now they look worried as they ask me how Tom is and, perhaps more importantly for them, how I am.

At first I am determined that I will be honest with people. I soon find, however, that honesty is not something most people can stand. They ask me how Tom is and, when I reply that he is dying or in terrible pain, they look away, change the subject or try to tell me it will all turn out OK in the end, which it won't. As T. S. Eliot says, we cannot cope with 'very much reality'.[1] So I try to be honest, but only with those I think can bear to hear it.

They ask me the same, anxious question, expressed in twenty different ways. It is most clearly articulated by our local funeral director, as we are walking together one morning towards a grave for a burial. 'What is this doing to your faith, Alan?' he says. I ask myself the same question. Like Job in the Bible, I cry out to God for an answer. I pray and plead and try to bargain, but like so much of Job's experience, and that of countless others, I find God is silent.[2]

I ask myself: 'What is the bottom line? What **can** I believe now?'

At first I think of a verse our local Methodist minister, also called Alan and a good mate, is fond of quoting: 'Love never fails.' It is from that most famous of passages about love, from St Paul's first letter to the Church at Corinth (another version translates it as: 'Love never ends').[3] As I ache with love for Tom and the anguish of seeing him in pain and the dread of losing him, I cannot believe that even death can overcome or destroy the power of this love. I am not always St Paul's biggest fan, but he so often says things which ring true, are profound, powerful and eternal. To the Church in Rome, facing persecution, he writes: 'For I am convinced that neither death, nor life, nor angels, nor rulers, nor things present, nor things to come, nor powers, nor height, nor depth, nor anything else in all creation, will be able to separate us from the love of God in Christ Jesus our Lord.'[4]

For a while this is my bottom line: 'Love never ends.' It is reinforced by that stirring passage from the Song of Solomon, the Bible's sensuous love song:

> Set me as a seal upon your heart,
>   as a seal upon your arm;
> for love is stronger than death,
>   passion fiercer than the grave.
> Its flashes are flashes of fire,
>   a raging flame.
> Many waters cannot quench love,
>   neither can floods drown it.
> If one offered for love
>   all the wealth of one's house,
>   it would be utterly scorned.[5]

Love will surely survive even death. And even death will not be able to overcome it.

That conviction does not last. I am not an optimist by nature. This is exacerbated by being from Yorkshire, where people don't like to get ahead of themselves or think too positively. They are stoic, expecting the worst. I remember sitting my A level exams, many years ago. We would queue up outside the gym before each exam, waiting to be let in. Just before we went in, my friend Brian would turn to me and say the same thing, every time. He'd say, in a very matter-of-fact voice: 'Soon be dead.' It seemed to sum up the Yorkshire attitude to life. 'Life is tough, so take it on the chin and prepare for the worst.' Well, maybe it is my Yorkshire roots or maybe I am just a natural melancholic. Whatever it is, sadly, 'love never ends', in my psyche at least, most of the time is not an answer I can cling on to.

What if love *does* end? What if everything ends with death? What if God is, as Professor Richard Dawkins insists, just a human invention, created to fit our need for meaning, hope and significance? What if there is no God? What if death is, indeed, the end? I am back again to the same question: 'What is this doing to your faith, Alan?' What is the bottom line, for me?

Later, after Tom's death, I go through a long period when I cannot engage with this question. I am too low, too grieved, too depressed. After he is dead there is nothing to do. All the medical equipment, the medicines, the special mattress, his Zimmer frame, the syringe driver, have been returned. Our daughters have gone to both live in Nottingham and there is no longer the daily round of doctors, nurses and other visitors. I do bits and pieces but I am in no condition to take on a full load of pastoral work or leadership. I am not sure what clinical depression is like, but I must be very near it. I sit in the bay window and think to myself: 'I will never get up, or move from here, or speak to anyone, ever again.'

My wife and I are very different characters. I feel entirely empty. She feels full: overwhelmed, overflowing with grief, loss, anger and pain. Her emotions are very near the surface. I cannot bear my own pain, never mind Annie's. It is all I can do to put one foot in front of the other. If she weeps, all I want to do is leave the room. It is no surprise to me that over 80 per cent of marriages, where there is the loss of a child, end in divorce. Our grief overwhelms us, and neither has anything to offer the other.

Unlike Annie, I feel empty and hollow inside. Numb. I have heard it said that depression is anger turned in upon oneself. Maybe that is what is happening to me. I feel myself closing down and sinking into depression. I sit on the window seat at home, looking out on to the garden as first autumn and then winter set in. Leaves fall and die. Everything is cold and bare, reflecting my mood. Beyond the garden, the rows of council houses, each holding their own problems, their own needs, look back at the vicarage where the vicar has nothing to offer them. 'What is this doing to your faith, Alan?' they repeat. For which read: 'If you go down, Alan, what will happen to the rest of us?'

6

Visit

Our children have always enjoyed a very close relationship with my parents. During our ten years in South America my mum never fails to write, every week, not just in general, but to each of our four children individually. They send presents, most of which never arrive – 'lost' in the Argentine and Bolivian postal systems. We only rarely have telephone contact but we record tapes to send to each other. Grandma tells us the news and Grandad tells stories for the children. Stories of Robin Hood and Little John, made up on the spot. They include a number of unlikely characters, such as Fatty Fudge who, in episode 34, is subject to attacks of flatulence, which our kids find hilarious. Grandma, however, the moral compass of the family, turns to Grandad with a sharp: 'Ronnie!' The story is then amended, so that what they actually heard turned out to be, not flatulence, but a squeaky floorboard, followed by a gas leak. They can't wait for episode 35.

When we first came home on leave we spent months living with them in their home. Tom was born while we were there. So there has always been a special bond between Tom and his grandma and grandad.

Grandad died three years previously. Before he died, though Mum was obviously struggling with her memory, they were coping OK. Six weeks after his death, however, we have an urgent, late-night phone call from Ruth, Mum's wonderful next door neighbour. At 11 p.m. she hears a noise. It is someone calling. It is my mum, wandering down her back garden, in the middle of the night, searching and calling out for my dad.

Thus begins the long and painful process of coping with dementia. Despite living 150 miles from Leeds, in Cambridge, we are the nearest close family. My only brother lives in Germany. Ruth, though, visits three, four, five times a day. Gradually she takes on all Mum's shopping, washing, cleaning, clearing up the mess, cooking and sorting out her medication. She does not do it for money – indeed she refuses to receive anything for her troubles. She does it simply because she loves my mum, her neighbour of 35 years. Without her, Mum would have had to go into residential care several years earlier, but because of Ruth, this self-effacing, generous, warm-hearted, godly woman, Mum is able to stay in her own home.

But what to do now? How will Mum cope with the news that Tom is dying? Will she understand it? I have already told her Tom is very unwell and has cancer. She shakes her head and looks down. 'Poor lad,' she says, 'poor Tom.' Tom has asked to see his beloved grandma. On the one hand, if we arrange for her to come down and see him before he dies, how will she react? On the other hand, don't Tom and his grandma have the right to see each other one last time? These are not easy questions.

Often when I visit Mum she announces: 'Oh – you've just missed our Lily!' Lily was her older sister, whom she was very close to, but Lily has been dead for two years. I gently remind her: 'No, Mum. Don't you remember? Lily sadly died a while back.' She looks utterly grief-stricken and cries out: 'Oh, no! Not Lily! Not Lily!' as if she has just heard the news of her death for the first time.

After a while I cease to correct her and talk about something else instead, such as the utterly heartless, door-to-door utilities salesmen who come and ask her, in a charming sort of way, if she'd like to save money on her gas and electric. 'Thank you. That would be lovely,' she says. The first I know about it is the final demand for payment which I find stuffed in the bottom drawer of the bureau. They have changed her service provider, but have not been able to switch the direct debit my dad set up before he died. So the bills are sent, but she just stuffs them in a drawer without realizing that she needs to pay them, which she has never had to do before. When I ring the companies they assure me they have a contract which she has signed – though they cannot, unfortunately, seem to find it or send me a copy. On another occasion they say she has entered into a 'verbal contract'. This happens several times. I put notices on her door and contact the utility companies, Age Concern, Help the Aged and her MP, but nothing seems to stop this cruel practice. Scottish Power finally offers a semi-apology. They tell me it was a rogue employee, who is no longer working for the company – not their fault, nor their policy, of course – but it is a nightmare to sort out.

I digress.

One of the things happening to me – and to Annie and the rest of us – is that my normal levels of tolerance have fallen dramatically. Things we usually take in our stride now become big deals. We are constantly at the edge of our ability to cope. Very close to our 'flash point'. We have never been a household for angry rows, but now small things trigger off big blow-ups. Anger is a very common symptom of grief. Looking back now, I can see that I had a lot of anger inside me, which I didn't recognize at the time but which was directed towards people close to me in unhelpful ways. Towards my brother, for example. He finds the whole situation extremely painful and has tried his best to help. He has paid for us to install Sky TV so that Tom can watch the sport when he is well enough. I talk to my brother on the phone about bringing my mum down to Cambridge to see Tom. His view is very clear. This would be a big mistake. She won't understand what's going on. She won't remember what has happened. It will just upset her, so why do it? He is insistent. He is trying his best to be helpful, but it only serves to make me furious. We have a row on the phone – which later erupts into a much bigger, extremely bitter row with Annie, partly at least, on the subject of why I bothered to consult my brother in the first place. We are at breaking point. Is this the end of our marriage? I am at my wits' end, unable to cope. I cannot bear Annie's anger and her distress. Feelings I think I've sorted, controlled, dealt with years ago, come flooding to the surface. I don't know what my breaking point is, but I am sure I am pretty close to it. I have always thought of myself as emotionally robust, but not now. My emotions are shot.

Our other children see me broken, weeping, distraught, at the end of my tether. They have never seen me like this before. I have always been the strong one, dependable, the solid rock beneath their feet, but now I am sinking in the quicksand. So are they, but unlike before, in their need and grief, I can no longer help them.

Tom is extremely unwell. He is in bed, sleeping fitfully or dozing much of the time, never comfortable. His voice has almost gone. We finally decide Tom has a right to see his grandma before he dies. I drive up to Leeds and bring her down. We sit in the kitchen and have a cuppa for her to recover from the journey. Then we slowly climb the stairs to his bedroom. He lies there, on his side, under his maroon blanket, bloated from heavy doses of steroids, exhausted by pain and the constant flow of morphine from the syringe driver. Grandma sits on the bed. 'Poor lad,' she says, tears in her eyes, 'poor lad.' Tom says nothing, but after a while, a hand slowly reaches out from under the blanket and takes hold of her hand. Tom lies there, the tumours everywhere, devouring him. His body spent, overwhelmed, dying. His mind numbed by the battle between pain and painkillers. Grandma sits there, confused, elderly, frail, and struggling to come to terms with what is happening. All that joins them are two fragile hands, held together in tender, silent embrace.

I think of the poem by Philip Larkin, 'An Arundel Tomb'.[1] It is about an earl and countess, portrayed in stone on top of their tomb. The earl's gauntleted hands seem firmly clasped together, but then Larkin notices that, in fact, the earl's right hand is only holding the gauntlet of the left. The left hand itself, withdrawn from the gauntlet, is at his side, tenderly holding his wife's hand. Centuries of snow, rain and wind have eroded the detail. They are almost unrecognizable. Only one thing remains of their weathered features. Like the weathered features of Tom and his grandma, as they sit, silently, side by side, on his death-bed, hand in hand. As the last line of Larkin's poem reminds us:

What will survive of us is love.

Baroness Sheila Hollins' daughter was left paralysed after being stabbed in an apparently random attack. She slowly learns to communicate by blinking out letters with her eyes, the only things she can move. One day she blinks out:

Body silent.
Inside love sings.[2]

7

Help

We are deeply grieved, struggling to cope, but we are not alone.

We are not alone in our suffering. Our friend Vivien comes to see Tom. She, too, is suffering from terminal cancer, though it is in remission. She, too, will die, in just a couple of years' time, leaving behind a husband and two teenage children. If you live in the Global South you expect suffering as part of life: poverty, hunger, disease, untimely death, war. It is not that these things are less painful for those who live in extreme poverty, war zones or refugee camps, but there is often, in such situations, a solidarity of suffering that is seen as part of normal life, accepted along with life's joys. Like Job, who says to his wife, after disaster strikes: 'Shall we receive the good at the hand of the LORD and not accept the bad as well?'[1]

In the West, instead there is a sort of unspoken myth that goes something like this: 'If you make the right choices and keep your nose clean, you can enjoy a great life, keep fit and well, meet the perfect partner, produce your 2.4 children (who also grow up happy and well, excel at school, get great jobs and in turn meet ideal partners), have a wonderful, rewarding career, enjoy retirement and, finally, die peacefully and contentedly in your sleep at the age of 95.' But it is a lie! I don't know anyone like that. Everyone suffers. The so-called 'normal life' includes tragic loss, family breakdown, childlessness, serious illness, domestic violence, redundancy, bankruptcy, mental illness, failure, disappointment, serious accident and a host of other painful, traumatic events. Yet, in the West, when suffering comes upon us, we often think it is an anomaly. Imagining we are the only ones, we ask: 'Why me?' Too often we find no solidarity in our suffering; rather, we find painful isolation. Vivien, however, does not ask: 'Why me?' but 'Why *not* me.' She, and others, bring us solidarity in our suffering.

The medical and nursing teams in the neurology, oncology and surgical departments at the hospital are also all doing their level best for us. The community nurses, who come in to look after Tom, are excellent. Pippa Corrie, Tom's consultant oncologist, and Stephen Barclay, our own GP, in particular, are wonderfully able, deeply caring, compassionate human beings. Reports that the NHS is going down the pan certainly do not match our experience. I think of our time in South America, where poor families we knew had to choose between taking a sick child to the doctor or buying food for the other children. Most could never have afforded the sort of treatment Tom is receiving. *We* could never have afforded the sort of treatment Tom is receiving. Mercifully those choices do not face us. We thank God for the NHS.

Also, Tom is not alone. He has good mates. Four *great* mates in particular. Like him they are awkward, 21–year-olds, not quite at ease with themselves in the adult world as yet. They have been mates for some time, since early days at Parkside Community College. All are quiet types, like Tom. None is a high-flyer. There are things you can measure by public examination, such as GCSEs and A levels, and things you can't. Things like loyalty, generosity, courage, determination, stickability, good humour, compassion, care, love. All of these things Tom has in abundance – and so do the great mates.

It is not easy to sit with someone who is dying. It is, for many people, quite unbearable. Jesus in the garden of Gethsemane the night before he dies asks his disciples to watch and pray with him for one hour, but they can't.[2] It is too difficult. They are overwhelmed with grief and they fall asleep. I know how they feel. Doing practical jobs is OK, but sitting with Tom and watching him die is torture. I can hardly bear it. Thank God that at least other members of the family are a lot better at it than me.

The great mates can face it – and do. Stephen, our GP, offers to meet with them separately. He explains to them what is happening to Tom and how best they can help him – mainly just by being there. They continue to visit Tom, regularly. They even come and sit with his body after he has died. Phil, Simon, Matthew and Daniel – thank you.

There are others, too. Tom is a great *Star Wars* fan, but he has been too ill to see the latest movie. Someone gets in touch with the Cambridge Picturehouse on his behalf and, through a string of contacts, they manage to ship over from America the reel of film and put on a special, private viewing of *Attack of the Clones* just for Tom and his mates, free of charge. He is not at all well but he is determined to go – and go he does. At the end of it he is utterly spent, and falls down the stairs on the way out of the cinema – but he has been to see it!

Despite what we had hoped, there is no remission. Tom is in no condition to travel in the UK, never mind abroad. We get in touch with Andrea at Lunn Poly and explain that we clearly cannot go to Crete after all. We wonder whether it might be possible to get at least a partial refund? She is incredibly kind and says she'll do what she can. Within a week she has resold the holiday and reimbursed us, almost in full.

Tom walks to the loo one night, supported by his Zimmer frame. Unfortunately he stumbles and the syringe driver, which is slung around his shoulder, crashes into the toilet bowl and stops working. It is a tragic, and also comic, scene. We get him back to bed and ring the emergency number we've been given. He needs that constant infusion of morphine or he will be overwhelmed with intolerable pain. By 2 a.m. the emergency technical team have arrived, replaced the syringe driver with a new one, set it up and taken the old one away. So many people, often in quiet and unassuming ways, have helped us in our hour of need.

People say to us, 'Just let me know if there is anything we can do to help' but, for the most part, we are too caught up with Tom's care to know what we need. In any case, we haven't the energy to pick up the phone, but some people don't need to be asked. They seem to know and they just do it. Shirley turns up, time and again, with a hot meal. People come round and just sit with us, listen to us. Others send us money – which, actually, helps a lot. Ank, my wonderful curate, and other people in the church, take over the burden of my work in the parish. The church as a supportive community is much underrated. They care about us, deeply. The diocese pays for me to have some counselling, though I don't know how much good it does. I just sit there, for most of the sessions, saying nothing, until the counsellor informs me that we have five minutes left and asks how I'd like to use the time. I have no idea!

Annie's best friend, Mary, whom she has known since they were in the Methodist Youth Group together as teenagers, turns out to be a rock. My mate Michael turns up, or rings up, and says: 'Hargrave, get your butt in the car, we're playing golf' and we play golf – Michael, Archie and me. There is something about hitting the ball which lets out some of the anger, pain and frustration I have no words for. Unlike Annie I am not someone who can cry easily. People say: 'Don't be afraid of having a good cry.' I don't think I am afraid of having a good cry. I often wish I *could* cry. It would be a release. It is like feeling nauseated all the time, knowing that if only you could vomit you'd feel better. I do not, as far as I know, try to hold it in, but I have no idea how to turn on the tap – or even where the tap is. So, instead, I play golf – once, twice, sometimes three times a week – and, months later, I am finally able to begin pouring out my grief to Michael. Only years later do I discover that, throughout Tom's illness and death, Michael was going through a really difficult time himself, but he never mentioned it to me. He knew how great my burden was and he knew I couldn't carry his as well.

Unlike some who, when they ask you how Tom is and you tell them, then proceed to tell you all *their* problems, *their* illness, *their* loss. So we become wary about whom we talk to, knowing that, right now, we can't cope with anyone else's pain on top of our own. Indeed, as Annie says one day, after she's read a passage from Isaiah about God's Suffering Servant bearing the grief and sickness of the whole world,[3] 'Well! I don't know how he can manage all that. We can't even bear our own grief, never mind anyone else's.'

It is no good, when you find yourself in a mess, to think: 'Oh! I must find myself some mates.' Or: 'I wish I lived nearer my family.' Strong relationships are like money in the bank. You can only draw on it if you've got it. One of the things I later come to value about Ely Cathedral is the Benedictine tradition. For many centuries Ely was a Benedictine monastery. One of the vows Benedictines take is Stability – something St Benedict, in his Rule, is very hot on. Staying in the same place. Living with the same bunch of people. Sticking at it through thick and thin. Not giving up. Working at the relationships, including – and especially – with the people you find most difficult, the ones who get right up your left nostril!

Increased mobility, however, people going off to university and never coming back, a flexible and international job market, means that stability is something we have lost over the last 50 years or so in a very big way. There is no putting the stopper back in the bottle, though. We are not all going back to live in villages where everyone knows each other. Yet we can build, for ourselves and for others, strong, stable relationships. We can invest in them, prioritize them. Take decisions which reinforce them rather than break them up. So that, when we need them – and when they need us – they are there. We didn't really realize it at the time, but we soon discover that, when it comes to strong, stable, supportive relationships, we are very fortunate indeed – and deeply blessed – to have a *lot* of money in the bank.

Michael Mayne speaks of seeing signs of God's kingdom, which are to be found and celebrated, not just in the Church, but all around us in the world.[4] Watching the news and reading the papers you could be forgiven for thinking that everyone is corrupt, selfish, on the make or downright evil, but it's not true. There are living signs of God's kingdom everywhere, and an awful lot of them, people of all faiths and none, have gathered around us in our hour of need.

8

The Ryder Cup

Flashback. 3 December 2000. It is my fiftieth birthday. Annie and I have been to the matinee at the Arts Theatre and now we are heading to a pub in Fen Ditton, presumably where the kids are waiting for us with a 'surprise' meal. However, it is a bigger surprise than I have expected, with over 50 people, family and friends, here to celebrate the big occasion. My brother has come over from Germany and has brought Mum down from Leeds. There is an old school friend I haven't seen for over 30 years. I am quite overwhelmed and completely fail to follow my own advice at such times: 'If you can't think what to say, don't say anything.' Instead, I ramble on for ages and tell a rather inappropriate joke that falls completely flat. Anyway, it's my birthday, so they all forgive me.

Now it's time for the presents, of which there are a considerable number, all shapes and sizes. My brother has bought me a cracking new set of golf clubs. Tom hands me a small envelope. In it there is a birthday card – to me and Annie for our fiftieth birthdays – and a letter. The letter is acceptance of payment for two tickets for the Ryder Cup at The Belfry, in Birmingham, September 2001. The tickets, it says, will be forwarded later. They are for the whole event – the three days of the tournament itself, plus three practice days. The price has been blacked out, but I know these are very expensive tickets indeed. Later that night, I am ashamed to say, I cannot resist holding the letter up to the light. The price is £400. It is typical of Tom's extreme generosity, shown in so many ways, though he is still a student, working only part time.

But September 2001 will not be remembered for the Ryder Cup. It is, instead, engraved in our minds for ever as '9/11', when terrorists flew passenger planes into the Twin Towers in New York and into the Pentagon. So the Ryder Cup is cancelled – or, rather, postponed – until September 2002, which is when my son, Tom, is lying at home in bed, dying.

Annie and I decide not to mention it. Maybe Tom will forget about it and we'll just not go – or perhaps we'll quietly give the tickets to someone else. Tom has not forgotten; the Ryder Cup is at the forefront of his mind. This is the one thing he still has to look forward to. He is really animated, longing for us to go. 'But what if something happens while we are away?' we plead, not wanting to say directly that the 'something' might be Tom's death. 'Not to worry,' he whispers, struggling with the tumour on his vocal chords, 'Liz is here, with Jo and Ben. They can look after me. Liz will ring you if anything happens.'

It seems we have no choice. We cannot deprive Tom of his dying wish. So we arrange to stay with our friend, Peggy, in Birmingham. We miss the first practice day – we cannot face leaving that soon. We set off on the Tuesday afternoon and arrive at Peggy's looking pale and exhausted. Wednesday morning dawns with grim foreboding. We don't want to go – but we know we must. We get dressed, sit on the bed and have a weep. Then we set off. We follow the signs to the course, park the car and go through the security check. Security is, understandably, incredibly tight. No cameras – and no mobile phones. No way of getting in touch until we get back home in the evening. We head for the entrance with thousands of others. They can't wait. Unlike us they are in high spirits. We finally arrive on the golf course, feeling as if we'd rather be anywhere but here.

But here is where we are and we gradually start to get into it. The practice days turn out to be a really good way of getting to know how to watch golf. Watching golf at a major tournament is not straightforward. We have never done it before. It isn't like football, rugby or cricket, where you find your allocated seat and sit there for the whole match. You have choices. Should you follow a particular group of players round? If so, you get the continuity of a single match, but you might never get a really good view of play, because of all the people who are already standing or sitting in the best places when you arrive at each new hole. Do you instead find a seat at an interesting hole and stay there, watching all the matches go through? If you do that, you may want to change halfway through the day to get a different experience and be at one of the later holes when the matches draw near to a conclusion. Either way, beware! Don't sit *too* near the end! A lot of matches will be finished by hole 15 or 16, so if you are on hole 18, you'll miss them completely!

We have a wander around all the holes, to see which are the most interesting and which provide the best views – sometimes views of more than one hole. After a while we work out our strategy. Hole 3 at first, a risk and reward par 5, where we have an excellent view of the approach shots over water and of the putting green. Then hole 15, by which time the matches are at a crucial stage. We don't stick to it religiously, but it seems to work pretty well.

We get back to the car and ring home. All is well – or at least no worse than when we left. We arrive back at Peggy's and begin to feel the relief of being away from the constant anguish of watching Tom die.

Friday morning dawns with no change in Tom's condition. The tournament proper starts today and we are beginning to feel excited. We find our way to the grandstand at hole 3 and settle down to wait. Colin Montgomerie is in majestic form. Why has he never reproduced it in a major? The Europeans surge ahead, only to be pulled back by the Americans. By Saturday night it is eight points all, with just the singles to come. High drama! Tom still OK.

We arrive on Sunday morning for the singles, full of hope and excitement, yet knowing that the Americans almost always win the singles. We get the playlist. Sam Torrance, the European captain, has front-loaded – all our best players are out first. The Americans have done the opposite, with world number one, Tiger Woods, playing in the last match. By the time he is on the back nine it will all be over and his match will be irrelevant. The turning point comes when Phillip Price, whose only previous claim to fame was being named Man of Pontypridd 1994, thrashes the world number two Phil Mickelson by three shots. Paul McGinley sinks the winning putt, is thrown by his fellow team members into a lake, and Europe have won a stunning victory.

We drive home in a state of high excitement. It is the best present we have ever received and the finest, most exciting sporting event we have ever witnessed – by a mile. We sneak in late, not wishing to wake Tom, who is on heavy doses of morphine and is dozing by 7 or 8 p.m. most days – but he is awake. He has forced himself to stay up and he wants to hear all about it. He is utterly delighted that we enjoyed it so much. I think it is the last thing he ever really enjoys and Annie and I feel rested, refreshed and strengthened for the days ahead.

We will need it, for Tom will die the following week.

9

End

There is a final, short walk by the river, all of us at Tom's side, watchful and attentive lest he fall. After a hundred yards or so we take a long rest. Tom can barely make it back to the car.

He begins to deteriorate rapidly. He can scarcely walk. His strength is spent, but he is determined. He makes one last, huge effort, late at night, supported by his Zimmer frame, to walk the ten yards from his bedroom to the toilet, body quaking. On reaching the loo, though, he stumbles and reaches out for support. Unfortunately the support he reaches for is the loo roll holder, which snaps off the wall. He stumbles and falls heavily on to the toilet bowl. We struggle to get him back to his bedroom. He will not get up from his bed again.

Care happens in a number of ways. It comes in the regular routine of the community nurses inspecting Tom's dressings and reloading the syringe driver. It comes in the visits of Stephen, our GP, who spends time with Tom, on his own, as well as with the rest of us, on our own, aware of our very different needs. It comes with Pat, Annie's GP, who sets aside time to be with her on a regular basis. It comes in the unexpected visit of a physiotherapist. She is a young woman from New Zealand, working and travelling over here for a year. She sits with Tom, talks with him. Then she rubs oil on to his thin arms and legs and gently massages them. The fragrance of the oil fills the room. It is a profoundly moving and sensual experience. Like Mary, who, despite the protests about her extravagance and sensuality, according to the Gospels, anoints Jesus to prepare him for his death.[1]

Tom is unconscious now all of the time. We take it in turns to sit with him. We are exhausted. Exhausted physically and exhausted with grief. A Marie Curie nurse comes in for the night to sit with him. She assures us that she will call us if he deteriorates further. We at last get some sleep. It is a welcome respite.

The following morning dawns and Tom is clearly slipping away. We all sit with him, crowded around his bed, listening to his rattling breath, shallow and uncertain. I hold his hand under the blanket and gradually feel it getting colder and colder. Try as I might I cannot keep it warm. The cold spreads up from his fingertips, through his hands, up his arms, into the core of his body. His body is still, unmoving, apart from his heaving chest. There is one, last, laboured breath, and he is gone.

We sit with him, and with each other, for a long time, over-whelmed with grief. Then we ring Stephen, our GP. He is teaching but will come as soon as he can. We are in no rush. Stephen loved and cared for Tom in life. We do not wish for anyone else to care for him in death.

Together we carefully remove all the machinery Tom is plugged into. We gently wash him and dress him in his best suit. We find a photo of us all, together with his beloved grandma and grandad, and slip it into his pocket. We, too, have cared for him in life and now we care for him in death. Sadly, these days, such cathartic rituals have largely been lost, as medical personnel and funeral directors carry out the tasks the family would once have undertaken. Like the women who loved Jesus, coming to the tomb on that first Easter day to anoint him for burial – only to discover that his body was gone.[2] We have been privileged to care for Tom's body in life and in death.

Later, Richard, our local funeral director, arrives to take Tom's body away. Over the next few days people come and remove his special mattress, the Zimmer frame, the syringe driver. We go to the chemist with a huge bag of medicines, including a large stock of morphine and codeine tablets. I cannot help wondering how much they would be worth on the black market. His room, so full of people, equipment and activity until very recently, is now empty and silent, just like the rest of us.

He is gone.

10

Farewell

John, one of our bishops, who has visited Tom on a couple
of occasions, comes to see us to talk about the funeral, which
we have asked him to take. We tell him we want the funeral
to have dignity, authenticity and honesty. No platitudes or
bullshit please. We definitely *don't* want that popular, Scott
Holland poem which falsely affirms: 'Death is nothing at all.'
The Bishop asks us about Tom's life. We relive a number of
anecdotes from his childhood and teenage years. Each of us
has different memories to share. His *Bottom*[1] sense of humour.
His witty remarks. His love of sport. His loyalty and steadfast
love for those closest to him. His quiet steadiness and ability to
rejoice in the success of others. His great generosity. His huge
courage in adversity. One thing we talk about is how, even
when he was desperately ill, Tom was concerned not just for
himself, but for others too. How were *we* coping? How *would*
we cope?

The Bishop asks me what he should wear for the funeral.
'Oh,' I reply, 'whatever you like. Nothing fancy.' I am interrupted
by a loud chorus from our kids. 'No way!' they say. They are
insistent that, for Tom, only the best is good enough. They want
the full works: embroidered robes, sparkly gowns, mitre, staff,
rings and anything else he can think of. Nothing else will do! It
has to be the best possible send-off. Holy Cross, where I am the
vicar and where the funeral will take place, is used for children's
clubs, dancing, our MP's surgery, St John Ambulance Cadets,
lunch clubs and other community activities during the week.
For worship on Sunday, the folding doors at the end are drawn

back to reveal a rather ordinary altar and cross. This is no Ely Cathedral. This is a pragmatic, 1960s, oblong box of a building, with nothing aesthetically pleasing to commend it, but that will be offset by having the Bishop, dressed in all his finery, robes shimmering in the flickering light of the fluorescent ceiling strips, which we can't reach to replace.

There is another painful row about whether Grandma should be at the funeral. In the end we drive up and bring her down. She is very confused. The day before the funeral, while we are all upstairs or out, she thinks we've gone to the funeral without her. So she wanders outside and falls in the road, banging her head. A neighbour finds her and helps her back home. She has a black eye but is otherwise, mercifully, OK.

On the morning of the funeral, Tom's coffin is brought to our house. When the time comes, we walk behind the coffin the short distance from our house to the church, next door. The whole place is heaving with people. All the seats are full. Many more are standing. Some people have travelled for many miles. Sainsbury's have closed the bakery, where Tom worked, for the day and some of Tom's colleagues are here. It is one of the many kindnesses of Sainsbury's and their staff.

The coffin is carried in to the theme music from *Star Wars*. The great mates have prepared a tribute, which they ask my friend Michael to read for them. Annie and I have also written thanks and tributes. In case we are unable speak, we have our friends, Mary and Alan, standing with us, supporting us, ready to take over if need be. The knowledge that they are with us, alongside us, gives us the strength to speak. Then the Bishop speaks. We sing our all-occasion, 'family' hymn: 'Guide me, O Thou Great Redeemer'. Then the prayers, during which the repeating chorus of a Taizé chant echoes around the room:

Within our darkest night,
You kindle a fire that never dies away,
Never dies away.[2]

Bishop John commends Tom to God's mercy and prays God's blessing upon us. Then, just as the coffin is lifted, there is the soaring sound of 'Gabriel's Oboe' from the film *The Mission*. We walk out, past the tear-stained faces of so very many people who love us, and head for the crematorium.

The following day we set off for Yorkshire. Ever since I was a child I remember going, with my Grandma Hargrave, the only one in the family to own a car, on trips to the Dales. My brother and I, with Grandma and her great friend, Aunty Annie, singing 'She'll be coming round the mountain when she comes' at the top of our voices as we drive down Otley Chevin, at a steady 25 mph. A favourite stopping place is Fewston Reservoir. It feels like a place we belong. Our roots are here. Three years ago we went there to scatter my dad's ashes, in the deep water of the reservoir. Now we are heading there again, to scatter Tom's ashes. We will scatter my mum's there when she dies, a couple of years from now, and hopefully one day, our ashes will go there too. We make a joke about a future BBC *Look North* news report of a strange, white island which has appeared near the shore of the reservoir.

There has been a drought, so we have to climb over a low wall and walk a fair way to the water's edge. We struggle to carry Grandma in her wheelchair, but she seems to enjoy the ride. Ben carefully pours the ashes into the water, I read some words of committal and we throw roses where the ashes have sunk, waiting until the wind carries them beyond our sight. It is a cold, overcast day, but then, just for a moment, the sun comes out. Mostly, I am too cynical to think of it as a sign, yet I can't stop the words of Julian of Norwich ringing in my head: 'All shall be well, and all shall be well, and all manner of thing shall be well.'

11

KBO

Let us prepare for winter. The sun has turned away from us and the nest of summer lies broken in a tree. Life slips through our fingers and, as darkness gathers, our hands grow cold. It is time to go inside. It is time for reflection and resonance. It is time for contemplation. Let us go inside.[1]

Winter. The cold, the bareness of the trees and the darkness reflect my mood. Getting on with life is not easy. It requires an enormous act of will to get out of bed each morning and face each new day. Snow falls heavily on the ground.

Ben goes out early one morning and arrives back late. He has been to Wandlebury, one of the few hills near Cambridge and surrounded by woodland. It is an area we often walked with the children when they were young. Until, that is, one autumn, when a severe storm uprooted, and even snapped off like matches, many of the beeches. It looked like a war zone and afterwards we did not return for a long time, but now Ben has returned. Beyond the car park and below the woods is an open, sloping field, grassland, covered inches deep with virgin snow. He sets to work. The curved back. The foetal pose. The beard and the bald head. The bloated features. Captured perfectly in snow. Tom, lying on his deathbed. How else would an artist express his grief? He stays with it for a long time and takes some photos to show us. Then, as the sun rises and warms the earth, the snow sculpture melts and sinks back into the ground. Ashes to ashes. Dust to dust. Without a trace. Like Tom himself, gone from our sight.

Spring is returning. Snowdrops push their way up through the hard ground and shyly open their green–white, drooping heads. Something inside me wants to go out in my boots and stamp them down, crush them into the ground, push them back down into the cold earth, so that I might remain here, in the cold, barren winter, frozen in time, like Miss Havisham,[2] for ever. But it is not possible. Inexorably, more bulbs spring up. Buds appear on the roses and the soft fruit bushes. Blue tits fly in and out of the nesting box. There is no holding them back. No stopping them. The irrepressible cycle of life goes on.

We watch a TV series, *The Gathering Storm*, portraying Winston Churchill, played by Albert Finney, in the years between the wars. Feeling powerless, he sinks into a deep depression: his Black Dog. His wife, Clementine (Vanessa Redgrave), appeals to his reserves of courage and determination with the phrase: 'KBO, my dear, KBO.' (Keep buggering on, my dear. Keep buggering on.) It becomes our own code word for struggling on with life when all seems bleak and pointless. I come downstairs, looking grim, paralysed by a bottomless well of sadness, grief and anger. 'KBO, my dear,' says Annie, gently. So we keep buggering on. It is all we can do.

People ask how we are doing. We quickly discover that most of them do not actually want to know. They cannot bear the truth. They need us to tell them that we are fine. That we are bearing up well. That faith is as strong as ever. That we are 'getting over it' – whatever that means. We try to be honest, but we learn to limit that honesty to a relatively small group of people who genuinely want to know and who can bear it, with us. Sometimes, for a while at least, they even bear it for us.

It is not helpful, but I cannot help it. I go over and over in my mind what might have caused it. Melanoma. Skin cancer. They never found a mark on his skin, nor even in his eyes, where it sometimes, apparently, starts. Neverthless, that doesn't mean it wasn't caused by exposure to the sun. Who exposed him to the sun? We did, going off to South America when he was just six months old. We did use sunscreen – though occasionally we forgot. La Paz is 12,000 feet above sea level so, despite being in the tropics, it is not hot, never getting above 25 degrees, but the air is thin so it is easy to burn, and burn badly, even on a cold day. The altitude? Did that contribute to his illness? It certainly didn't help. What about the salmonella infection? Surely he'd never have got salmonella if we'd stayed in England? The treatment: 'Enterolit', the recommended treatment for stomach infections in Bolivia, containing heavy doses of chloramphenicol, an antibiotic used only as a last resort in the UK. Did that irreparably damage his immune system? If we had stayed in the UK, would Tom have still been alive? Is his death all our fault?

We agonize over these questions, for which have no clear answer. Despite the well-meaning insistence of others that it probably didn't make any difference, the truth is that, although we never knowingly took decisions we thought would hurt our children, we may well have been responsible for Tom's death.

With such thoughts in my head, I play golf.

Annie runs. I do not think she runs because she enjoys running, certainly not now. She runs because she cannot help herself. She runs in order to survive. She runs to where she can be alone with her thoughts, her grief. Pounding the towpath and the fenland tracks is all she can do. She is not yet able to return to her work as a psychotherapist, so what she has on her hands is time. If you are going to run distances, time is what you need. You need to spend hours running, which is exactly what she does.

She has only taken up running recently. She does a short Fun Run. (Fun Runners – such an inappropriate term. They don't do it for fun. They may not be fast, but they are *serious* runners.) Then she manages 5 km, a significant milestone. She hopes to make 10 km – that will be her limit, she says. Then she runs 10 km. She can never run a marathon, she assures us, but she begins to believe that she might, just possibly, be able to run a half-marathon – 13 miles. Before he dies she talks to Tom about it. She tells him she will run the Great North Run, a half-marathon, in his honour. She will raise money for Macmillan. She sends off the application form and, a few weeks later, to her surprise, a letter arrives, telling her she has got a place.

It is easy to see why charities such as Macmillan, Cancer Research UK, the British Heart Foundation, Marie Curie, local hospices and many others are so strongly supported, or even set up, by people who have had to face those same challenges in life. There is something redemptive about 'giving something back'. Hoping that you might prevent – or at least alleviate – the suffering of others. Affirming that your own suffering has not been in vain. That this is not just a fluke of chance in an arbitrary universe, which has neither purpose nor meaning. Affirming instead that there *is* a purpose. That, though you would never choose it, good can, perhaps, come out of suffering.

Annie has put in the miles, got herself the place and started to raise money. Thank God for JustGiving, an online giving site, who do all the money collecting for you. There are few things more dispiriting than nagging people to pay up the sponsorship money they have promised, after the event. I announce it in church and invite people to sponsor Annie. After the service ten-year-old Samantha comes up to her and holds out a fiver. 'This is for the Run,' she says. Samantha is standing there with her younger brother, whom she cares for. She also cares for her mum, who is an alcoholic, mostly incapable of looking after herself, never mind the kids. Annie looks at the money and then at Samantha. What to do? This is the money her mum has given her to buy lunch for them both at McDonald's, across the road. If she takes Samantha's money, they will have no lunch, but how can you refuse such a generous, precious, costly gift?

Then she has a moment of inspiration. In her other hand Samantha is holding a cross, which she has made in Sunday Club. It consists of two pieces of wood, held together by string with Jesus, a paper cut-out, graphically coloured in with plenty of blood, tied to it. 'Actually,' says Annie, smiling at Samantha, 'I think I am doing OK for money, but what would really help me is that cross. I could take it with me, to the Run. Could I possibly have your cross instead?' Samantha's face lights up with a beaming smile. She puts the money back in her pocket and hands over the cross. Annie thanks her warmly.

That cross becomes very important for us. It is the cross of suffering and pain. I cannot even begin to think about resurrection. I cannot bear the thought of a glorious, victorious God in heaven, but I can just about bear the thought of a God who comes down to Earth, who takes on human form, lives our life, grows up in the carpenter's shop, works in the family business, enjoys a drink with his mates, goes to weddings, becomes famous and popular for a while, then suffers rejection, betrayal by one of his closest friends, desertion and denial by the rest, a mock trial, flogging that rips the flesh off his back in chunks, and a cruel, agonizing death, hanging, gasping for breath, on a cross. The God who knows what it is like to lose a son – an only son in his case. This is a God who knows what it is like to suffer. This is the only God I can relate to just now, in any shape or form.

Annie carries the cross with her up to Newcastle. She carries it to the starting line. Then she hands it to me and carries it in her heart instead, alongside Tom. She runs the Great North Run in a T-shirt bearing a picture of Tom with the words: 'This is for you, Tom'. We see her off, straining to spot her among the 20,000 others as they pass by, then we head for the finish. We finally find her, exhausted and exhilarated, at the end of the run. Despite all her protestations at the time, 18 months later she will run the London Marathon. She will raise a heap of cash for Macmillan. It does not bring Tom back, but it is redemption, of a kind. That is not why she runs, though. She runs because she cannot help herself. The medals, and the cross, still hang proudly on our wall.

Running for Macmillan

A certificate
A prize
A medal
To put up on the shelf
To hang up on the wall
One of the top three highest fundraisers
With many thanks for your commitment to helping
Macmillan improve the lives of people with cancer.
A certificate
A prize
A medal
But no son
To be proud of me.[3]

She continues to run. I continue to play golf. We keep buggering on.

12

Back to work

Over the course of Tom's illness I have gradually been doing less and less work. I am fortunate that, as a vicar, I am pretty much free to do as much or as little as I feel able to. I am also extremely blessed in having a curate, Ank, who, with others from the church, quietly bears the load of pastoral care, of funerals, of children's activities, of worship, without burdening me.

Two or three weeks after the funeral, Annie and I turn up for church on Sunday and sit at the back, silently weeping our way through the service. At the end of the service Pete, someone we hardly know, but who has clearly heard all about us, comes up behind us and lays his hands heavily on our heads and shoulders. He prays fervently, in a loud, cheery voice, thanking God for victory over death, praying that the Holy Spirit would fall upon us with power and that everything would turn out OK and we'd go on our way rejoicing. He means well, but I cannot bear it. My anger surges to the surface. If I had the strength I'd get up and deck him! It reminds me of a passage from Primo Levi's profound book about his experience in a Nazi concentration camp during the war.[1] There has been an arbitrary selection of people for the gas chamber. A young man, with a wife and children, who knows he will die tomorrow, lies on his bed, weeping. Meanwhile, an old man, called Kuhn, sits on the next bed, rocking back and forth in prayer, loudly thanking God that he has been spared. 'If I were God,' says Primo Levi, 'I would spit on Kuhn's prayer!' That's how I feel about Pete's prayer, too.

Most people are kind, respectful and thoughtful. They do not try to change us or the fact of Tom's death. Rather, they sit and weep with us.

A week or two later, I turn up for an evening service. It is an occasional act of worship called 'Adults Only'. The idea is to eat together, to be creative, to tackle issues current in people's lives and to allow time for discussion. It is a small group led, this time, by one of our ordinands – trainee vicars on placement with us. He talks about pain and suffering, but then reads a passage from the Bible which says that, despite the suffering, everything will turn out hunky-dory in the end. 'Well,' he asks, looking round at us, expectantly, smiling, 'what is our response to that?' No one says anything. I tell myself to not say anything either. 'If you can't say anything helpful, Alan, don't say anything at all.' It certainly wouldn't be helpful. I remind myself: 'You are the vicar, so just let it pass. Don't take your feelings out on this poor guy who is inexperienced and doing his best.' I shouldn't have come. I am not ready for this yet. It is all too raw. I wait. I count to 60. I bite my lip. In the end, the silence is too much for me. I cannot bear it. I cannot keep it in. The anger wells up and overwhelms me. So, finally, I blurt it out, saying: 'It's complete bullshit.' Just as I thought, it isn't helpful. There is a stunned silence. No one knows what to say. After a while I walk out and go home.

Annie is a psychotherapist with an organization offering integrated health care to those working in the international mission, aid and development sectors. Many of her clients have had deeply traumatic experiences. She will be in no condition to work with them for many months to come. Her employers are understanding. She is given compassionate leave. She receives a full salary for a while. Then half. Then nothing. More than half our income has now disappeared. It is not something you think about, but suddenly, just when you are at your most vulnerable and needy, you find yourself facing not just serious illness, death and grief, but financial problems as well. Many, in similar situations, end up in very serious financial difficulties indeed.

Being a vicar is not well paid, but at least there are fringe benefits. No one ever suggests that I shouldn't be paid in full. Furthermore we live in a house provided by the Church, so there is no mortgage or rent to pay. The Bishop sends us some money, for a holiday. Friends also help in a variety of ways. A couple we used to work with in Argentina, but haven't seen for years, send us £1000 in the post, quite out of the blue. Financially, thank God, unlike many people in our situation, we will be OK.

I gradually start to get back to work. I do the easy things first. I go to a community meeting. Pop in to our local infant school. Things I enjoy and which do not take a lot out of me emotionally. I begin to think I could, perhaps, manage a funeral. The funeral director rings me about an elderly woman from the parish who has died, Mrs Frost. She leaves a husband and two adult daughters, both of whom live in Cambridge. It sounds pretty straightforward. I decide not to pass it on to Ank this time. I'll do it myself.

I turn up at the house of one of the daughters, where Mr Frost is staying for the time being. His other daughter is also there. I check the deceased's name, age (87) and the date and time of the funeral. We sort out hymns and readings and I begin to ask about her life. They've been married for over 60 years. It turns out she has had heart and other serious health problems since her early sixties. Papworth Hospital fitted a pacemaker and later on did by-pass surgery, which extended her life by 25 years. She has had a good innings. But her husband is clearly very agitated. Then, without warning, he blurts out, in a loud voice: 'It's so unfair! So unfair!' Then he wails: 'Why? Why?' Instead of gratitude for their 25 bonus years together, he feels bitter and aggrieved. All he can think of is how unfair it all seems, how alone he now is, how badly done by. I feel the anger well up again within me. I look straight at him: 'You ungrateful old sod! How dare you complain! You don't know how bloody lucky you are! She lived for 87 years. Eighty-seven! Not 21, like my son! So don't give me your pathetic, self-indulgent: "Why?"!'

This time I manage to control my anger. I say this to myself. To him I say, with all the sympathy I can muster, which isn't much: 'I am so very sorry.' I go home, deeply shaken.

The following week I decide to do some pastoral visiting. I book three visits in my diary. People I know well who are lonely and would appreciate a visit. Not difficult visits. Betty is first up. She is a small, elderly woman with a big personality who has had a difficult life. She lives in the back room of a council house, heated by a single paraffin heater to save money. She is eccentric, but I like her a lot. Almost every time I go to see her she hands me a grimy, old envelope. Inside are several ten- and twenty-pound notes. 'This is for the pipeline,' she says, in a low voice, meaning the water project our church is supporting in Uganda. She has given me over £1000 for this project during the past year alone, all saved from her pension, but this time there is no envelope. She wades straight in. She says, angrily: 'Why didn't you go and see Elsie before she died?' 'Well,' I begin, 'to be honest I've not really been much in circulation, as you know. Ank went to see her – and, in any case, she was a Catholic and the Catholic priest has been to see her.' She is not to be put off so easily. She states categorically that I am the vicar, this is my parish and I should have gone – and that's that. I start to become angry myself and can scarcely restrain myself from retaliating and saying something, to this generous, faithful, frail, if some-times difficult, elderly woman, that I might deeply regret. I leave under a cloud, feeling dreadful. I can't face the other two visits. I am drained and exhausted. I go straight back home instead.

As an adult I have often reflected on how fortunate I was to have such loving and supportive parents and extended family. They provided a solid foundation that has given me consider-able inner strength – and I have needed it. Some years ago, when I was a curate, the vicar was diagnosed with Parkinson's disease. At about the same time his marriage broke down. His emotional turmoil and worsening health were, for better or worse, played out in the church community. It meant that what had been a large, thriving, confident congregation began to flounder. As I stand at the door of the church one Sunday morning, greeting people as they leave, Margery, a member of the congregation, grasps my hand fiercely and says: 'Thank God for you, Alan! You've got strength enough for us all!' At first I am flattered, but, gradually, I begin to see what a lie it is. Now, years later, after Tom's death, any remaining thoughts of being strong have gone. I am no longer robust. I am shattered, broken. Now it is my turn to see my personal turmoil and tragedy being played out in public, in a different church and a different community. I have tried to love and minister to people on this council estate parish on the edge of Cambridge for over ten years, but now it seems to me like a bottomless pit of need, overwhelming me. I know that I simply cannot meet that need any more.

13

Moving on

———•·◆·•———

I begin to realize that I need to move. I also know that most of the people who support me, who support us, who have been our lifeblood this past year or so, live in or around Cambridge. So we do not want to move too far. I make an appointment to see the Bishop to talk about my future. I explain my situation and ask if he knows of anything which might be suitable in the area. 'Well,' he says, his eyes lighting up, 'what about the Canon Missioner's job here at the cathedral?'

I am not looking for a cathedral job so I had not noticed the advert. Although I love the building, I have always thought of cathedrals as places of privilege, elitism and establishment. Not my style at all. 'Oh, I don't think a cathedral job is for me,' I reply. 'Why not?' he says. 'At least, have a look at the job specification. It could be just the thing for you.' We chat for a bit longer and then I head home. Without enthusiasm, more to please the Bishop than anything else, I ring up the cathedral and ask them to send me the details. When the pack arrives, a couple of days later, I read through it with growing excitement. 'Bloody hell!' I say to myself. 'This is my dream job!' As I look back at my ministry in South America and in the UK over the past 20-odd years, it all seems to be so relevant. It has all, in one way or another, been focused on mission. Mission to address the pressing social and economic needs of indigenous people in northern Argentina. Mission to plant churches and make disciples in Bolivia. Mission to start a new church, on a council estate, in Cambridge. Mission to our local schools. Mission to the underdog, to prisoners, to the forgotten, to people who think of themselves as rubbish, but who are precious and beloved in the eyes of God. Could such a view of mission be transferred to a cathedral? It certainly seems to be what they are looking for, according to the job description. I hardly dare believe it, but in my heart I feel that everything I've done so far in my life has prepared me for this moment. There is only one way to find out. I fill in the forms and send them off.

To my surprise I am called for interview. It is a two-day affair. A tour of the cathedral, lunch with senior staff and a presentation to give on Day One. Dinner with the Cathedral Chapter and the Bishop that evening. Wives are invited. Best behaviour. Try not to eat too fast and don't slop the gravy down your shirt! Day Two is a series of interviews with the Bishop, Dean and other Chapter members.

I start to prepare the presentation. I do a bit of research about cathedrals from their websites. I am shocked to find that, although they all include virtual tours, none of them seems to connect spirituality to the building and its history. I have done a bit of this sort of thing myself at the Leper Chapel, built to serve the needs of a leper hospital on the edge of Cambridge in the late eleventh century. It is in my parish and I find that its history – of those who were thought to be beyond the pale – ill, disfigured and forcibly separated from their loved ones – seems to ring bells with many in my parish who themselves feel 'outcasts'. I arrange regular school visits to the chapel. Children and staff are often in tears as we light candles for those who are ill or dying, for those who feel rejected or excluded, for family members from whom they are separated, for dads they no longer see. Perhaps I could do something similar at Ely Cathedral, on a bigger scale? Could we use the building to make such connections for our visitors, so that they experience not just an historical tour but a spiritual pilgrimage? How can I present my ideas? I have never used PowerPoint before, but a mate from the General Synod gives me a quick overview. It turns out to be pretty easy and user-friendly, especially as most of my presentation will be pictures.

I turn up for Day One. There are five of us being interviewed. The others are all smartly dressed in black and speak with posh accents. They look like ideal cathedral material. At one point I am sitting with one of the other candidates' wives in the deanery dining room, waiting to be called for my presentation. We begin talking. 'We are just praying,' she says, with all sincerity, 'that the right person, the person God is calling, will be appointed.' I have had it with piety, though. 'Oh,' I reply, 'I'm praying that *I* get the job.' She is not impressed. At last I am called to give my presentation. It seems to go down OK. Annie joins me for the evening and, thankfully, I don't disgrace myself at dinner.

We get home at about 10 p.m. There is an answerphone message. It's from the City Council Works Department. They say that the tree is ready and will be going in at 9 a.m. tomorrow morning, if we'd like to be there. My heart sinks and I am thrown into turmoil.

We have talked, as a family, for some time about a memorial for Tom, a place to go and remember. We finally settle on having a bench down by the river, in the place he regularly walked our black Labrador, Princess Sheewana. She is named after a Larson Far Side cartoon, in which two dogs are introducing themselves over the garden fence. One says: 'I am Vexorg, Destroyer of Cats and this is my wife, Princess Sheewana, Barker of Great Annoyance and Stainer of Persian Rugs.' Having seen the cartoon, our kids settle on the name long before we ever get the dog. Anyway, it is in this place, where Tom walked, threw sticks in the river for Sheewana and filled his pockets with conkers every autumn, that we decide to put the bench. We also decide to plant a tree next to it – a horse chestnut, of course. That is why they've rung. They are planting the tree tomorrow morning at 9 a.m. and have invited us to come. It is at the exact time I have an interview with the Bishop.

What to do? Annie and I, with our son, Ben, sit up late, talking. Should I just forget the interviews? Wouldn't going to the interviews instead of the tree planting be, somehow, a denial of my love for Tom? I wrestle with my conflicting thoughts. In my mind is the passage about Jacob wrestling with the angel.[1] I have a postcard of the huge sculpture of this event, carved in marble by Jacob Epstein, which I have seen, recently, at Tate Britain. I sit and look at it. I notice that, actually, the sculpture captures the moment when the wrestling is over. Jacob's hip has been put out of joint and he can no longer stand upright. Jacob is spent and almost lifeless. They are no longer wrestling. Instead they are intimately held together, by the angel's powerful arms, which hold Jacob up. What is more, the limp body of Jacob looks remarkably like Tom. The wrestling is over for me as well. I can 'no longer' as the prayer[2] says 'stand upright', so I lie down on the bed, utterly spent.

Annie and Ben go to the tree planting. Ben has saved some white roses from Tom's coffin, which are now dried. He puts the petals carefully into the hole in the ground in which the tree is to be planted. He takes photos to show me and his sisters. The workmen are very supportive and respectful. It apparently all goes off well and the tree looks healthy, surrounded by its protective fence, overlooking the river. Annie asks the men if they will keep an eye on it for us. One of them smiles kindly and says: 'We'll do our best, love.'

Meanwhile, I have arrived at the Bishop's house, a reluctant interviewee, feeling dreadful. 'How are you this morning?' he enquires, cheerily. 'Terrible,' I reply. 'I almost didn't come.' Then I tell him about what has happened and my conflicting emotions. He is very supportive, but I am aware of not wanting to play the 'Tom sympathy card' and we move on to discuss other things. Given the circumstances, the day goes off, as Wallace might say to Gromit: 'as well as can be expected'. It is such a relief to head home. I feel completely wrung out.

Annie is on retreat and Ben is out, so I am on my own when the phone goes. It is the Dean who says, in a cheerful voice: 'Well, you've got the job!' I can't believe it. 'What are you going to do to celebrate?' he asks. It is not the reply he is expecting. 'I am completely knackered,' I say. 'I am going to bed.' I do at least remember to say thanks and that I am very pleased to accept the job. Then I head for bed. Tonight I will sleep well.

14

New life

The New Year is shattered by Grandma falling in her bedroom and breaking her hip. She will spend the next six months in St James's Hospital in Leeds. Over the next few weeks she undergoes three different operations. At one point it looks as if she has given up and is ready to die, but with a lot of medical intervention, she pulls through. The surgeon, surrounded by his housemen and medical students, tells me, in a confident voice, how successful the operations have been. I look at this frail, elderly woman, my own mum, suffering from dementia, now completely institutionalized, wheelchair-bound and unable to go home, and I wonder *why* they have gone to such lengths, such expense, to keep her alive?

When she leaves hospital, we move her to a nursing home near us in Cambridge. It is not at all how she would have wanted to end her days, yet I am not sure we could have coped with another death at this point in our lives.

I start to wake up in the middle of the night, not able to breathe. I sit on the edge of the bed, trying not to panic, thinking that maybe my lungs are full and I need to breathe out before I can breathe in. Usually, within twenty or thirty seconds the breathing begins to return to normal. I go away for a couple of nights, on retreat to Turvey Abbey, but again I wake up in the middle of the first night, unable to breathe. I sit on the bed, mouth open, gasping, but nothing happens. It goes on a lot longer than usual, for almost a minute. It is a frightening experience. When I finally get my breath back, I get in the car and drive to the A & E department at Bedford Hospital. I tell

57

them I think I've had an asthma attack, though I have never suffered from asthma. By now I am breathing normally again. They check me over thoroughly. My lung capacity is excellent and they can find nothing wrong. When I get back home I talk to Annie about it. She suggests it may well be psychosomatic, related to Tom's death. I am extremely sceptical. She would say that, wouldn't she? She is a psychotherapist, after all. Over the next few weeks or so it gradually goes away and I forget about it.

Ten years later, as I am sitting writing about Tom's death, a niggling pain begins in my left shoulder and gradually creeps up to my neck. It lingers, so I take some painkillers. I wonder if I have been sitting in a cold draught? It feels like a stiff neck. It is still there the following morning, only it has spread up the left side of my head. I take more painkillers but it doesn't go away. After three days and regular painkillers, it still hasn't gone away. I do not generally suffer from headaches, so I start to worry and begin to imagine all manner of possibilities. In the middle of the fourth night, at about 3 a.m., having tossed and turned, trying to ease the discomfort, I finally sit up, wide awake. I rub my neck and my head with my fingers, trying to feel exactly where the pain is located. It is very definitely focused on the left side of my head, above the ear, behind the eye. As I lie there, riddled with anxiety, it suddenly strikes me that this was exactly the place where Tom first experienced the pain in his head. Surely this cannot be a coincidence, can it? I think about Tom for some time. About his terrible headaches, far, far worse than my own. About the painkillers he takes, all in vain. I talk to him; I pray for him. Within ten minutes the pain is gone and does not return.

The following morning I tell Annie about it. She gives me a knowing look and says: 'You know what my colleague Evelyn[1] would say? She'd say: "We are fearfully and wonderfully made."'[2] Having just finished reading a book about the physical effects of emotional trauma on soldiers in the First World War,[3] even I have to admit that she may, after all, be right.

Annie and I go on holiday to Mexico, thanks to the generosity of friends. It is a cut-price package, as the Americans are hardly flying after 9/11 and they are desperate to fill up the hotels in Cancún. It has its difficult moments but we enjoy the sun, the food, Mayan temples, snorkelling, even each other. When we return the local hospice offers us counselling. We are both having counselling individually, but we begin to see Chris, a therapist offered to us by our local hospice, together. It is a safe place to say and hear hard things. She helps us a lot. Tentatively, we begin to be able to be intimate with each other again.

Jo goes on holiday as well. 'Anywhere but Tenerife,' she tells her friend, who is looking for a last-minute deal to book, but Tenerife it is. Standing with his mates at the bar one evening is a tall Spaniard. He smiles at Jo. She thinks to herself, to her own amazement and disbelief: 'I am going to marry that guy!' They meet. They talk. They fall in love. She comes back to England. They are on the phone every day. Antonio, who has never been beyond mainland Spain and doesn't speak English, gets on a plane and arrives in Nottingham. He gets a job. This is serious.

A few months later they arrange to come down to Cambridge for the weekend. They make sure all the rest of the family can make it. It is a warm, summer evening and we take the dining table outside into the back garden. After we've finished eating Jo says: 'We have an announcement.' We already know what it is. They are going to get married. Everyone is delighted. We drink a toast to Jo and Antonio. Then a toast to the grandchildren. This is backed up by Ben handing them a present – baby socks! We have had a few drinks by now. The party becomes raucous and hilarious. Each toast envisages an ever greater number of grandchildren. I propose a toast to the *eight* grandchildren! Annie gives me a look. It is ridiculous, she isn't even pregnant, but suddenly the thought of new life fills us with hope.

The wedding takes place the following April. Jo is the Bargain Queen. She buys her wedding dress in the January sales, slightly shop soiled, for only £50. It costs her more to have it dry-cleaned.

A beautiful pair of shoes: £2 from Oxfam. She makes her own veil and books the University Sports and Social Club for the reception. They decide to do without an official photographer. It is a good move as, within a few days of the wedding, they have hundreds of excellent digital pictures sent by friends, some of whom are keen photographers (though, of course, there are none of Tom, who, in our photo albums, remains 21 years old for ever).

A few weeks before the big day Jo announces that all caterers are complete rip-off merchants! So she has decided to do the catering herself – at our house. 'Not to worry,' she assures us, 'it will not mean any extra work for you!' Actually, it turns out to be an excellent move. Antonio's mum, grandma and sister come over a few days before the wedding and it gives us all a common task, which everyone enjoys, in which to share as we get to know each other. I take Jo to the church in our own car, a red Mazda Demio, silver ribbon draped across the bonnet, tooting and waving at everyone we pass. Jo's godfather, David, the retired Bishop of Argentina, conducts the wedding wonderfully well in both English and Spanish.

It is a beautiful, joyous occasion. We arrive at the reception. The food is excellent. The music starts. We begin to dance. I had not realized what an excellent dancer Ben is, dancing Flamenco with the Spanish relatives. Then, somehow, the five of us are on the floor: Annie, Liz, Jo, Ben and I. We are holding on to one another, arms around each other, in a circle, dancing, leaping, laughing, shouting for joy together at the tops of our voices. I never thought I would really be able to laugh or celebrate again, ever, but here we are, enjoying ourselves without reservation, without restraint, without a shadow. It is a new beginning. We are able to live and laugh and love again.

The wounds have not gone away, of course. We are more fragile now, more fearful. Instead of Tom's death making us feel that we have had our share of bad luck and all will be well from now on, it has the opposite effect. We have become acutely aware of all the dangers life holds.

Ben goes off to Bolivia to work for several months in a children's home. We are anxious about him, especially when he emails to say he is walking the Taquesi Trail. This is an old Inca pathway across a mountain pass from La Paz to Chulumani in the lowlands. I walked it myself, years ago. The trail itself is OK, apart from the effects of high altitude at the top of the pass, which is about 16,000 feet above sea level. Coming back on the bus, along the 'road of death', is another matter, however. It is a single track, cut into the mountainside, with vertical drops and nowhere to pass oncoming vehicles. There are also regular landslides. There are crosses and flowers, every few hundred yards, marking the places where vehicles have gone over the edge. 'Please God, not Ben as well.'

He gets back safely to La Paz and his time in Bolivia finally comes to an end, but on the way home he misses his flight in Lima. He manages to phone us. He may be able to get a flight tomorrow, he is not sure. He will ring again and let us know. Hours go by. There is no phone call. Lima is not a place to be on your own at the best of times, even less so with no money. We imagine, in detail, all manner of terrible things which are probably happening to him right now. He has, no doubt, been taken into Lima by an unscrupulous taxi driver, beaten, robbed and left for dead. We are worried sick.

My mobile phone goes. My body tenses. It is not him. A day and a half later, the phone goes again. At last it is Ben, who announces, in a big, cheery voice, that he is in Madrid and should be in London in a couple of hours. Apparently there was a last-minute seat on a flight to Spain and no time to find a call box before the flight. He is glad to be back, but we are all shattered.

Later, Liz, who by now has bought herself a house, announces that she and her partner, Colin, are expecting a baby. It is wonderful news, bringing new life into the family, a new generation. The pregnancy is far from straightforward, however. The doctors fail to recognize the symptoms of eclampsia. Mid-delivery, she is rushed in for an emergency Caesarean section. This is life-threatening, as we know only too well. 'Not again, O God. Please, I beg you, not Liz!'

I don't know why I bother to pray. It doesn't seem to do any good, but I cannot help myself. I feel like Simon Peter. When the going gets tough and many of Jesus' followers start to desert him, he turns to his twelve disciples and asks them: 'Do you also want to abandon me?' Peter answers, perhaps more in desperation than in faith: 'Lord, who else can we turn to?' Like Peter, I have nowhere else to turn.

In the film *Shadowlands*, when his wife is dying, C. S. Lewis is asked by a friend why he continues to pray, if God doesn't answer his prayers. He replies, 'That's not why I pray. I pray because I can't help myself. I pray because I'm helpless. I pray because the need flows out of me all the time, waking and sleeping. It doesn't change God. It changes me.'

It is touch and go for some time, but then Liz begins to pull through and starts the long, slow road to recovery. Joshua is born. Not a substitute for Tom, but precious new life. Another generation. We cradle him in our arms and bring our faces close to him, breathing in deeply the warm fragrance of newborn baby. This precious, fragile bundle of love. Joshua Thomas is born and hope is born again, too.

As the saying goes: 'Life's too short.' Yes it is, and there is a strong feeling now that we must all live each day to the full, be thankful for it and make the most of it – not just for ourselves but for others too. I hear the haunting words of Ewan MacColl's 'Ballad of Accounting' ringing in my head. As I think about poverty, the refugee crisis, global injustice, he asks me: 'What change did *you* make?'[4] MacColl was a communist, an agitator for workers' rights, one of the leaders of the 'mass trespass' movement which led to the moorlands and hills being opened to the general public. So, now we try to live each day as a gift; live each day as if it were our last. For we know, from experience, that it could well be.

I think about what it means to 'get over it'. It certainly doesn't mean, for me at least, feeling as if it had never happened. That would be a complete denial of Tom and of our love for him. I still feel the loss. It often catches me unawares, when my guard is down. In the supermarket I spot someone who, from behind, looks exactly like Tom. Someone uses a phrase that is just what Tom would have said. England win the Ashes, but there is no Tom to enjoy it with. Father's day, there are cards from Ben, Jo and Liz, but no over-the-top present from Tom. Getting over it is not about not feeling the loss. It is, perhaps, about not being paralysed, immobilized, debilitated by grief any more. It is about being able to live again.

We *are* starting to live again. Indeed, we feel gratitude. We have suffered a grievous loss, but we also have so very much to be thankful for.

15

Leaving

———◦◦◦◦———

Breaking the news to people at Holy Cross is not easy. It plays on my mind right from the moment I'm told I've got the job. I am not at liberty to tell anyone until the clearances are done and it is publicly announced – not for about a month. On the first Sunday morning there is a united service at the Baptist Church. It is not that far away, only half a mile from home, but I have some books and props to take for the service and in any case it is a bitterly cold February day, so I take the car. The service finishes at about 12 and I hang around, chatting to people and drinking coffee, but my mind is on other things. Certainly not on the service at the Baptist Church and not, either, on the fact that I have asked our son, Ben, to pick up Annie in our car, at 12 noon from Ely, where she has been on retreat since Friday.

Ben goes out at 11.30 a.m. to drive to Ely and pick up Annie, but the car is not there. Neither has he any idea where I am. He assumes I will be back soon so he waits. I am not back soon. I don't get home until 12.30 p.m., to be met by a very agitated Ben who asks me what I am playing at and where on earth have I been. Then it hits me! I jump back in the car and race to Ely at top speed.

When I reach the cathedral, at 1 p.m., there is an arctic wind blowing from the east. They say there is nothing between Ely and Siberia, and today it certainly feels like it. In front of the cathedral, shivering, alone, stands Annie. She has been there for over an hour, in the freezing cold. I open the door and tell her I am so sorry. She gets in. She is far too cold and far too livid to speak. Forgiveness is still a long way off. I have not seen her since I got the job, but now is not the moment for congratulations. Ice is not just a physical thing, and it takes a fair while to thaw out. This will not be the only cock-up over the next few weeks, as I live with my mind in at least two places at once.

I have taken over as chaplain to the Cambridge Air Cadets, which is on the edge of my parish. I have been doing it for a few months now, but my official swearing-in as chaplain will be this coming week, at the airport. The Regional Chaplain makes a speech in which he thanks me most warmly for taking on this important role and hopes I will stay for many years to come. I feel like a complete heel as I come forward, shake his hand and receive my badge of office, knowing that, in three months' time, I'll be gone.

Apart from the family, the first person I tell is John, our wonderful church warden. He is a Norfolk man: slow, considered and deliberate in his speech. As I tell him the news I see the tears well up in his eyes. He looks into my face. 'I think it is just the right thing for you and the family,' he says, with typical generosity, 'but, personally, I am completely gutted.'

The following Sunday I announce it to the church. I give out the notices at the beginning of the service and then say: 'There is something else I have to tell you now which is difficult for me to say and will probably be difficult for you to hear as well. I have been appointed Canon Missioner at Ely Cathedral and I'll be leaving after Easter.' There is a gasp of disbelief. A stunned silence. I open my mouth to say more, but no words come out. Tears roll down my cheeks. I look down at my feet. When I look up again I am surrounded by people, also in tears, hugging me, standing with me, holding me up, as they have done for many months now.

As I talk to people after the service it becomes clear that, though they are gutted that we are going, they are also proud since, as they see it, I am being promoted: 'Our boy done good!' One of them says: 'We thought you might go after all that has happened, but we couldn't have borne it if you'd just left us to move sideways to another parish.' I look at Samantha, who is ten years old and a lovely kid, despite her dire circumstances. She and her brother turn up regularly on a Sunday morning at 8.30 a.m., an hour and a half before the service starts. They wait for me to open the door. They scavenge the kitchen for any leftover food and I always try to make sure there is some. They often haven't eaten since their free school lunch on the Friday. She looks utterly crestfallen at the news and I feel I have betrayed her – and the rest of them as well.

Three months later we do leave. The church has gone all out, inviting people from far and near to the farewell service and the party afterwards. There are hymns and readings. I give a farewell address. They have commissioned a family of puppets, specially made – one of them the spitting image of me, dog collar, beard, glasses and all! Then they call us up to the front of the church. There is a prayer net on the wall, an old trawler net, to which we tie pieces of wool as a symbol of our prayers, for ourselves and for others. When we don't have the words to say, we do something symbolic instead, something beyond words, tying that person or situation into the patchwork of prayers, held before God, here in church. Over the years it has become a beautiful, coloured tapestry of our prayers. Annie and I are made to sit down, side by side, in front of the altar. Then they cut a large piece out of the prayer net and wrap it round us. Different people come forward and tie their piece of wool or ribbon into the net as they pray for us. It is a deeply moving act. They are binding themselves to us as we prepare to move on. We will carry it with us, this symbol of their love for us, wherever we go.

I arrange a short sabbatical between leaving Holy Cross and starting work at Ely Cathedral. Part of it is a two-week trip to Ireland with my Methodist minister friend, also called Alan, who has just started his sabbatical. Our visit, to quote Alan, is to be 'pilgrimage-light' – visiting holy sites, those 'thin places', and climbing Croagh Patrick – but also enjoying the coastal scenery,

Irish stew and pints of Guinness. As we travel around the north and west coast we are struck by the raw beauty of the coastline, but also by the many famine pits, containing the bodies of the countless thousands who died in the potato famine of the 1840s, to the callous indifference of the British hierarchy. We imagine, as we sit on rocks by the shore, at the end of the land, desperate families, crammed aboard vessels bound for America. The 'End of the Land' becomes an important metaphor for us. Alan's sabbatical has been blighted by the tragic death of his uncle and cousin in a freak boating accident on the Donegal coast. The end of the land is a place of tragic loss. A place of departure. A place of stepping out, into an unknown future.

The end of the land will come unexpectedly
Without malice
As an onshore wind will build a swell
And, rising over a sand bar,
On a turning tide
A breaking wave will swamp a boat.

And two men
Loved for giving life and living it well
Will have theirs smothered
By the heartless waters
Of the Western Approaches.

The icy embrace of these depths
Will be a cold, cold shock
For those at home
Who suspect nothing.
For our stark grief, tears will not do.
Only a deep wailing will be enough.

Great raw rising waves of sadness will overwhelm us now
The heartless waters of the Western Approaches

Reach much too far inland
And break on new shores.
The end of the land has come unexpectedly.[1]

16

The Grand Round

It is just over two years since Tom died. We see Stephen, our GP, from time to time. One day he talks to us about the fact that, despite all the pain we have faced as a family, we have, in his view, dealt with Tom's death openly and well. He and Pippa, Tom's oncologist, believe that others could benefit from hearing about Tom's care, not just from a medical but from a personal perspective. He tells us about the Grand Round – which sounds to us like a secret Masonic ritual. It turns out to be a weekly open meeting, at Addenbrooke's Hospital in Cambridge, for all the medical staff from any discipline who wish to attend. It lasts an hour and involves two presentations, of 20 minutes, each followed by 10 minutes of questions. Then there is a buffet lunch provided. He does not want to put us under any pressure and suggests we take some time to think about it and then contact him if we want to talk about it further.

There is something redemptive about the idea that our experience may be of help to others. So, after a lot of discussion, we agree to be involved. We meet with Stephen and Pippa and decide that it would be best for us all to speak, each in turn, taking up the narrative as it impinged on us personally. We decide to write a full script so we all know and are happy with what the others will say.[1] It will also make it easier to keep to time.

By chance, we have recently experienced the death of my mother, also in Addenbrooke's Hospital, following a severe stoke in the nursing home where she had lived for the past two years. Her excellent care, as she lay dying in hospital, and the very thoughtful and compassionate way in which a junior doctor told us what was happening and invited us to be involved in the decisions about her treatment, has also made us very thankful for the NHS. Part of what we want to say is, simply: 'Thank you.'

The big day comes and the lecture theatre is crammed with about 500 doctors, nurses and other healthcare professionals. The event is chaired by one of the professors, clearly a man who enjoys being in charge. First up is a research student studying Parkinson's disease. He is nervous – not helped by interjections from the professor. 'Come on, doctor,' he barks, 'get to the point. You've already had ten minutes and haven't told us anything new yet.' It does not bode well, but it also makes me determined not to be intimidated.

Our turn arrives. Stephen introduces the theme and we are under way. To our surprise people are very quiet and attentive. Mercifully the professor does not interrupt. Neither do we overrun. Annie and I talk about what, on the whole, has been a very positive experience of the NHS – swift to act, multi-disciplinary, skilled, caring and coordinated. We do have a few gripes – about not being listened to initially regarding Tom's vomiting reaction, about the use of language and about the undisguised enthusiasm among some medics when confronted with Tom's unusual presentation of melanoma – a fascinating case rather than a deeply painful human tragedy.

In the question slot at the end the professor, without realizing it, amply illustrates our point about not listening and using inappropriate language by saying to us: 'Well, of course, you were lucky. You had a very clear diagnosis.' I cannot believe what I am hearing. I turn to look at him. 'No,' I reply, firmly, 'we were extremely *unlucky*. Tom's diagnosis was not good news. It was terrible news. It was a death sentence.' There is what seems like a nod of understanding from most of the people in the lecture theatre. They, at least, do not miss the point.

17

Bottom line – 2

One of the questions the Dean asked me when I applied for the job at the cathedral was: 'If you get the job, how will you get on with having to come to Morning and Evening Prayer at the cathedral every day?' Founded by St Etheldreda in AD 673, Ely Cathedral was for many centuries a Benedictine monastery. The rhythm of life of the monks and nuns was defined by the seven daily acts of worship, the Daily Offices – the Opus Dei, meaning the Work of God. The real Work of God was not tending the garden, copying manuscripts, looking after the sick, welcoming guests, caring for the buildings or providing food. All of these were important. The real Work of God was the daily round of prayer and worship. These seven offices have now been reduced, in the Church of England at least, to two – Morning and Evening Prayer. So one of the essential tasks of cathedral clergy is to be committed to this daily rhythm of prayer and worship.

I think about the Dean's question. 'Well,' I reply, 'it is not what I have been used to, but I'll give it my best shot'. In fact, however, I find it to be liberating, like a homecoming. I have always struggled with my daily devotions, made worse by friends who tell me what a marvellous time of prayer they've had this morning and how God has spoken to them through their Bible reading. I can safely say that this has hardly ever been my experience. Now I don't need to decide what to do each day, however – there is a standard format to follow. It's not just me either. In the morning there are six or eight of us, gathered together to pray. I even find myself arriving ten or fifteen minutes early, just sitting, quietly, before the office begins. I am often distracted, thinking about my family, about my work, about the news headlines, about how Leeds United are doing, about the next game of golf. For me, it would be an exaggeration to call this 'prayer', but at least I am here, putting myself deliberately in God's presence, whether he chooses to reveal himself or not – which, generally speaking, as far as I can see, he doesn't. Yet there is something in this daily routine, undertaken with others, which makes me feel centred, held. Like Philip Larkin who, in his poem 'Churchgoing',[1] despite his own scepticism, cannot help affirming: 'It pleases me to sit in silence here.'

Each afternoon, when I am engrossed in my work, the last thing I want to do is break off and sit in a cold cathedral for Evensong, but I go. I listen to the familiar words of the liturgy and hear the Bible readings. The choir sings the canticles and an anthem, reflecting the beauty of this place and of God's extravagant creation. I hear the prayer requests of our visitors offered to God. Remarkably, despite my reluctance beforehand, I am stopped, stilled and refocused, ready for whatever the evening brings.

In particular, there is the chanting of the psalms, in the same way they have been sung for centuries, which forms the core of the Office. These psalms express to God every possible human emotion and desire. To quote the long-gone *News of the World*: 'All human life is there.' There is despair, anger, confusion, disappointment with God, complaint, bitterness, the desire for revenge. As the psalmist says bitterly to God (Psalm 44): 'All this has come upon us though we have not forgotten you or been false to your covenant. Wake up, O God! Why are you asleep? Do not cast us off for ever.' Also present, though, are thankfulness, joy, awe, praise, adoration, faith, hope and love, as in Psalm 126: 'Then was our mouth filled with laughter and our tongue with shouts of joy. The LORD has done great things for us and we rejoiced.' These psalms remind me that it is OK to express to God all these conflicting emotions, even at the same time. They say something profound about the deep paradoxes of life, including my highly contradictory feelings about my

relationship with God. Epstein's sculpture is not just God wrestling with Jacob, nor even with Tom. It is God wrestling with
me – if only, that is, I could get hold of him. George Herbert,
in his poem 'Bitter Sweet', sums up for me this internal conflict.

> Ah my deare angrie Lord,
> Since thou dost love, yet strike;
> Cast down, yet help afford;
> Sure I will do the like.
>
> I will complain, yet praise;
> I will bewail, approve:
> And all my sowre-sweet dayes
> I will lament, and love.[2]

'Lament and love.' That seems to sum up my existence.

The cathedral is helpful in other ways, too. The pace of life is
much more hectic, demanding. So many balls to keep in the air
at the same time. There are lots of exciting, innovative projects
in which I am involved. There is so much going on, every day.
It is non-stop. Now, however, I am generally one or even two
steps away from the 'coalface'. I am responsible for the 10,000
schoolchildren who visit here each year, but the work is deliv-
ered by Jan, our outstanding Education Officer, and her team
of volunteers. I only occasionally get directly involved with
the kids. Similarly, the Ministry of Welcome Team and the day
chaplains are the ones who actually do the work of welcoming and ministering to the general public. I simply manage the
wonderful Joan and Sally, who manage the rest of the team.
Also, one of the other cathedral canons is responsible for most
of the pastoral care, so I do not often, now, have to bear the
weight of other people's pain. It is a great mercy to me.

In any case, people here are different. In East Barnwell people
wear their hearts on their sleeves. For example, I meet Sharon
on the way to school with the kids. 'Morning, Sharon,' I say.
'How's things?' 'Bloody terrible,' she replies. 'Had a big row with

Mike. I gave him a slap. He gave me a slap. Now he's walked out and there's no money for the gas!' Whereas, at the cathedral, I say: 'Morning, Julia. How are you?' 'Oh, fine, thanks,' she replies, with a big smile, even though she is in the middle of a painful, acrimonious, messy divorce and is very far from being fine. I miss the honesty, the rawness, the 'craic', but I know in my heart that I just don't have the inner resources to meet so much need, to carry so much pain, any more. So, I am grateful for the cathedral, which holds me in the 'Cantus Firmus' and allows me to do what I can, not what I cannot.

The words of the funeral director still ring in my head: 'What is this doing to your faith, Alan?' So, what *do* I actually believe now? Also, as my emotions vary so much from day to day, is belief in God a completely subjective thing, dependent just on how I happen to be feeling at any given time? There are many days when I cannot honestly say that I believe in the existence of God at all. God is silent, distant. Maybe God does not even exist. What if God doesn't exist? What is the bottom line, then?

I think Christians, for far too long and even now, have focused unhelpfully on what we say we believe. Credal statements were written to define orthodoxy – and to exclude heretics. In our own day the Church seems determined to exhaust itself, and look ridiculous into the bargain, by arguing endlessly about issues of sexuality and gender. Yet the Gospels are comparatively silent when it comes to credal statements. For the most part, Jesus defines discipleship by trust in him and by what we do, rather than what we say we believe. Indeed, the very word 'faith' does not refer to a set of metaphysical propositions which I may, or may not, sign up to. Rather it means something more like 'risky faithfulness'. It is about how you live it out. This is well illustrated by the Quakers, who do not have a basis of faith, but have made a vast difference to society, over the centuries, by their faithful, committed work for justice, for honesty and integrity in business, for decent conditions for workers and prisoners, for peace and reconciliation.

Maybe the Churchills were right after all? 'KBO.' 'Keep bug-gering on.' Because, even if God does not exist, the values of the Gospels, the teaching of Jesus, the way of life which loves neighbour and stranger above self, which is committed to work for justice, for peace, for the powerless, for love to triumph over evil – these things are surely worth fighting for, whether God exists or not. So I will keep on 'buggering on', trying to live out Jesus' teaching as best I can, irrespective of how I feel, because this is a better way to live. Better for me. Better for my fam-ily and for the people I love. Better for society. Better for our nation. Better for the world. This is a bottom line I certainly *can* hold on to, whether God exists or not.

Just occasionally, there are also moments of serenity – the soaring music, the astonishing coincidence, the sense of it all fitting together, the look in the eyes of someone I meet – when I suddenly glimpse the glory of God again. In between those moments, I will do my best to walk the walk, both when God seems close and real and especially when he doesn't.

Another thing about working in the cathedral is the Communion of Saints. I have repeated, for years, this phrase, as I have recited, week after week, the Apostles' Creed: 'I believe in the Communion of Saints.' What does it mean? Does it have any importance, any cash value, for me, here and now? In the cathedral I am surrounded by saints – images in stone, wood, paint and stained glass. Images not just of distant heroes of the Bible, but of the saints of Ely. Those people who lived and prayed and walked and worked here, in this very place where I am sitting now. People like Etheldreda, the Saxon queen, who gave up crown and wealth to found the monastery here, in the middle of this bleak marshland, in AD 673. There is an almost tangible sense of not just the challenge of their example but also their presence and prayers for us today. 'Since we are sur-rounded by so great a cloud of witnesses,' says the letter to the Hebrews,[3] 'let us run with perseverance the race set before us.' It seems as if they, too, are calling to me: 'KBO, Alan, KBO.'

This Communion of Saints is not just about the saints of old. I think of all the godly people, the saints of today, who have supported me, supported us, over the years, both before and since Tom's death. Those who have held us, stood by us, stood for us, when we were unable to stand for ourselves and are supporting us still, now. I may often find it hard to encounter God directly, but I meet him all the time in people such as these.

Early one Friday morning, when I am playing golf, as usual, with Michael, he asks me: 'Does it give you any comfort, Alan, to think that Tom is safe in God's hands and that you will see him again?' It is a difficult question for me. 'To be honest Michael,' I reply, 'these days I have no assurance about what happens after death, much less whether I will ever see Tom again.' He stops and turns to look at me. 'Oh, Al,' he exclaims, 'don't worry about that! I believe passionately in life after death. I believe passionately that Tom is safe in God's loving arms and I am certain that you will see him again. If you can't believe it at the moment – don't worry – *I'll* believe it for you.'

What joyous relief! What deliverance from the unquestioned individualism of our age. Not to have to believe everything for myself! To be able to be part of the communion of saints, past and present, who will hold me, support me, pray for me and even believe for me, when I am spent, and can do none of it at all for myself.

One of the highlights of a visit to Ely Cathedral is the Octagon. Built after the collapse of the central tower in 1322, it is a miracle of medieval engineering. The monks worshipped directly underneath it. It was deliberately built eight-sided. The monks' rhythm of life was defined by a seven-day cycle of work and prayer. The eighth day represented eternity, into which they were drawn as they worshipped, lifted up by images of saints and angels into the heart of the octagon, where a painted carving of the risen, ascended Christ looks down upon us. He is holding up his right hand as a sign of blessing. With his left hand he is pulling open his clothing to reveal a deep, red-raw, open wound.

This image becomes very important for me. I read again the story of doubting Thomas who, when he finally meets the risen Jesus, recognizes him not so much by his risenness, but by his woundedness. Jesus says to Thomas: 'Reach out your hand and put it into my side. Do not doubt, but believe.'[4] The risen Jesus is not the same as before. He is deeply scarred, wounded. It is no surprise that many of his disciples do not initially recognize him when he appears to them. His appalling suffering has changed him. Then, as he ascends, he takes into heaven that deeply wounded body, so that God might always and for ever know what it is like to feel the pain and suffering of our wounded humanity.

Nicholas Wolterstorff, an American professor of philosophy and religion, in the profound book he wrote following the death of his son, Eric, in a climbing accident, comments on this passage: 'So I shall struggle to live the reality of Christ's rising and death's dying. In my living my son's dying will not be the last word. But as I rise up I bear the wounds of his death. My rising does not remove them. They mark me. And if you want to know who I am now, put your hand in.'[5]

Like Wolterstorff, like the wounded, risen Christ, I will rise up. I will live again, but I am not the same as I was before. If you want to know who I am now, put your hand in.

Name

When they came . . . the whole town was stirred because
of them
And the women said: Is this Naomi?
She said to them
'Call me no longer Naomi
Call me Mara[6]
For the Almighty has dealt bitterly with me.'

Gomer conceived and bore a daughter.
Then the Lord said:
'Name her Lo-ruhamah[7]
For I will no longer have pity . . . or forgive them.'

And when you ask me who I am
When you ask me if I am as I appear
I say
'You may still use my name of grace
But I am now called
One-who-has-lost-a-son
For I am marked by a grieving.'[8]

Jeanette Winterson, in her moving autobiography, says: 'Wounding seems to be a clue or a key to being human. There is value as well as agony.'[9] She may well be right but, frankly, I'd rather be without it and have Tom back, any day!

18

Blessed

———•◆•———

Birthdays come and go. More grandchildren are born: Lucia and Ximena. Grandchildren Tom will never know. Grandchildren who will never know Uncle Tom, though we regularly talk with them about him. He is part of our conversation. Part of the ongoing story of our lives. New people are added to our circle of family and friends. We grow older and change. The world changes. There is sorrow as well as joy: the tragic loss of baby Esther. Tom, though, remains the same. It is a strange paradox. He journeys on inside us. He is part of who we are. Yet he is always 21.

People give us books to read about coping with grief. Most of them are unfit for human consumption. They often depict people strengthened, renewed and rejoicing following their ordeal. The worst ones paint a God who 'loved Tom so much that he took him for himself'. What sort of despotic, despicable God is that? A God who treads roughshod over our love for our son and his love for us, and snatches him away, like some selfish ogre? Few books seem to face up to the reality of grief and death. Few books can stay with lament, with the suffering and pain of Good Friday. They always seem to want to rush on to Easter Sunday, to a victorious, happy ending, without the desolation, the silence, the nothingness of Holy Saturday. Without the ongoing, open wounds. Without appreciating that, without death, there can be no resurrection. There is resurrection, but it doesn't usually happen, for me at least, after only three days.

C. S. Lewis's *A Grief Observed*, an account of his wife's death is a welcome, if painful, exception – a raw and honest narrative

of the pain of the loss of his wife and of his struggle with faith.[1]
Another is a book already mentioned, Nicholas Wolterstorff's
Lament for a Son,[2] but these are rare exceptions.

September 2004 – another Ryder Cup. Europe's biggest ever
margin of victory: 18½ points to 9½. A brilliant performance
and a fantastic result. Bernhard Langer, the European captain,
when interviewed afterwards, says simply: 'We creamed 'em.'
Yet, the following week I feel terrible, plunged into a deep, dark
place of depression and anger. I cannot understand why. Then I
remember why. What happens the week after you win the Ryder
Cup? Answer: your son dies.

Three years on from Tom's death, Annie and I drive in to
Cambridge and park the car by the Green Dragon pub. We
walk across the footbridge and out along the path by the side
of the river until we reach Tom's tree and bench. We sit down
and look out over the river. Our view is partly obstructed by
a boat tied up a few feet away from us. As we sit, quietly, saying nothing, a kingfisher appears, perched on the bush to our
right. Then it flies down and perches on the mooring rope, just
in front of us, not more than ten feet away. Kingfishers are not
that rare, but to see one so close is extraordinary. Usually, all we
see is a flash of colour streaking low over the water, but now the
blue and gold of its feathers shimmer in the sunlight before us.
All our senses are heightened as we watch it dive down into the
river and then back up on to the rope, again and again. We sit
quietly, watching, waiting, for about 20 minutes. We feel privileged to be here. Our rational minds dismiss it, but it seems like
a visitation; a sign. These sorts of experiences are like glimpses
of God: glimpses of hope, of resurrection, of assurance. They
are rare, but they help sustain us. I am reminded of 'Folk Tale',
a poem by that grumpy, depressive Welshman, R. S. Thomas.
It is about prayer, based on the fairy tale of Rapunzel. He
imagines himself at the foot of a tall tower, throwing prayers,
like gravel, against a distant window, without any response. Yet
he concludes:

I would have refrained long since
but that peering once,
through my locked fingers,
I thought that I detected the movement
of a curtain.[3]

For me, too, very occasionally, I think I detect the movement of a curtain. That is just about enough.

Exactly a year later there is a knock on the door. It is my friend, Hugh. 'I've just come round to say that I am thinking of you especially today,' he says. He has remembered. I had forgotten.

In my work I meet others who have lost sons and daughters. Many are sudden deaths – accidents, suicide, murder. Deaths where the first thing you know is the policeman on the doorstep. No opportunity to say farewell. No opportunity to make things right. Sometimes they are deaths where the last word spoken has been a bitter one; where relationships are left unresolved, unhappy. Relationships which can never now be mended. People rightly fear cancer and the painful death it often brings. For Tom it was indeed a terrible, painful and untimely death. For us, too, it was pure agony and heartbreak, seeing him suffer, day after day. Yet I am deeply thankful for the time we were privileged to share with Tom, and with each other, through those dark days of his dying. We took the time to say all that needed to be said. We sat with him, cared for him, held him and were at his side as he breathed his last, leaving all else aside in that Sacrament of the Present Moment.[4] Such times are precious, important, of immense value. I do not in any way thank God for Tom's illness and death. I wish to God he were here with us now. I do, however, thank God for Tom's precious life and for time we spent together in the months of his dying – time with Tom and time with each other.

Tom's death has strengthened the bonds between us. This is not always the case. Grief can be destructive, a breaker of relationships. Often there is recrimination, anger, blame. Sometimes people are utterly crushed by loss and never recover. Few marriages survive the death of a child. We are lucky, blessed. Each of us, in different ways, receives ongoing support from a circle of people around us who love us and stick with us through thick and thin. 'Those friends thou hast, and their adoption tried, grapple them to thy soul with hoops of steel.'[5] Friends, colleagues, the church community, people in the medical and caring professions: they help us in practical ways, in listening to us and being with us, in remembering us and praying for us, in laughter and in re-engagement with the normality and the joy of living.

We are, for the most part, able to be open and honest with each other, though this is often far from easy. And we are, generally, not ashamed or afraid to ask for help. We are fortunate to be inheritors of good models of stable, strong relationships, from my parents in particular, which provide us with the commitment and belief to stick it out. We feel we owe it to Tom to make the best of the gift of life. Determined to love each other and to live as well as we can, as though each day were our last, trying to make a difference, for the better, that we ever lived at all. Unlike so many families, which end up torn apart, destroyed, by grief and death, we are lucky and blessed.

After Tom's death, Liz and Jo decide to live together. It is not just a short-term move. They still live within five minutes' walk of each other, in and out of each other's homes, now with their husbands and children. Ben decides to go to university in Nottingham, to be near his sisters, and stays there for several years. Though now in London, he is regularly back and forth. Annie and I will go and live in that same area when I retire, along with Shirley, another member of our family. 'Each other' is of huge importance. We often fail to realize just how important it is, until it is threatened or lost. More important than that attractive career move which takes you to the other side of the country, if not the world. More important than the lovely house you have seen, many miles away on the other side of town. For in the end 'We' are much more important than 'I'. Also, without

'We' there can be no meaningful 'I'. Rediscovering the importance of stability[6] and commitment in relationships has been, and is, a huge blessing to us.

Perhaps surprisingly, much of the time we are indeed thankful. Thankful for Tom's life. A life which is not just measured in years but in quality of relationships and in its lasting impact on us and on others. Would it have been better if he had never lived, and so spared us the pain and the grief of his death? Certainly not! I am profoundly grateful for our 21 years with Tom, for all the love and laughter and generosity he shared with us. Love and laughter and generosity that live on inside us and continue to bless us.

I recall hearing Desmond Tutu speaking in Cambridge, before the end of apartheid. He talked about standing with a family in Soweto, powerless to do anything, as a bulldozer smashed down the home where they had lived for many years. The home that contained all their worldly goods. As the house was crushed flat, he suggested they pray together, but, as this tragedy was happening, he could not think of anything to say. After a time of silence, the man whose home had just been destroyed prayed: 'We thank you, O God, that you love us.'

Thankfulness, gratitude, an ability to count one's blessings. Such attitudes are not always easy to foster, but they make a huge difference to how we experience life, even in the face of tragedy. Viktor Frankl, holocaust survivor and psychologist, insisted that how people coped with the concentration camp depended largely on their inner attitude, which was the only thing they could control.[7] We have a choice. We do not have to submit to bitterness, resentment and self-pity. George Herbert, the seventeenth-century clergyman and poet, wrote:

Thou that hast given so much to me
Give one thing more: a grateful heart.[8]

I am reminded, too, of Ernesto, whom we met, years ago, in Embarcación. He had been to the regional hospital in Salta, but they were unable to do anything for his cancer, so he was heading home to die. He stayed with us while waiting for a lift home to his tiny village, deep in the remote, semi-arid, Chaco area of northern Argentina. Annie asked him one day, as they ate breakfast together, if he had any children. 'Yes,' he replied, with a warm smile, 'one living and eight with the Lord.' Then he told her how the eight children had all died within a fortnight of each other during a measles epidemic. The only one living was born afterwards. Yet, far from being bitter, disappointed, resentful, he is thankful to God for his life and for his family. He is thankful, content and at peace within himself. He is patiently waiting for a truck to arrive. Waiting to go home to die. Waiting to go home to the 'land of the living',[9] where he is certain he will see them all again.

I do not think I am in denial of grief, or in denial of Tom's death or of other times of pain, loss and sorrow, which all of us must face in life. I am not always able to see it, but I have a great deal to be thankful for. A very great deal. I am richly blessed. So, I will strive to resist allowing bitterness, resentment, disappointment or anger to fester: things which ultimately destroy me and destroy my relationships with others. Instead I will seek to foster gratitude, to be thankful, to count my blessings. Because I am indeed richly blessed. Because, in any case, it is simply a better way to live.

10 October 2012, the tenth anniversary of Tom's death. Annie, Liz, Jo, Ben and I park the car and make our way across the footbridge. We walk along the footpath by the river, picking up conkers and putting them in our pockets, just as Tom would have done. The tree looks in good shape. It is, hopefully now, beyond the size at which it could easily be vandalized. We wonder how long it will be before it, too, produces conkers? Many years yet, I think. We stand by the river and throw in the roses we have brought, watching them float away, as the current gently carries them downstream, beyond our sight. We sit on the bench. There is just enough room for all five of us to fit, arms

around each other. We sit for a long time, saying nothing. There is no kingfisher today.

At last we get up to leave. Before we go, we take one long last look at the small brass plaque screwed on to the bench. It is tarnished and weathered. Why didn't we bring some brass polish? We always seem to forget it. Still, the engraved words are clear. It says all we need to say. In the end, all that remains of us is love.

In memory of
Tom Hargrave
1981–2002
We loved him and he loved us

Appendix

On dying at home, aged 21. Tom's story.
Addenbrooke's, 4 May 2005

STEPHEN

This is perhaps a slightly unusual case presentation for a medical staff round. The patient was a 21-year-old young man with metastatic melanoma: the presenters are myself, his GP, Pippa Corrie, his oncologist, and his parents, Annie and Alan Hargrave. The focus of this session will be the journey Tom, his family and friends, and his professional carers travelled after the diagnosis was made. In many staff round presentations, the diagnosis is the point of arrival; we are taking the diagnosis of incurable cancer as the point of departure.

By way of background, I will start by summarizing the events that led up to admission here. Annie and Alan will take the account on from there, with comments from Pippa and myself along the way, and we will leave five to ten minutes at the end for questions, perhaps questions in particular to Annie and Alan. While this is a deeply sad story, it raises issues that we all meet in our clinical practice, and our aim is to stimulate thought and reflection.

Tom was a 21-year-old single young man, who worked as a baker in Sainsbury's, and lived at home with his parents, Annie and Alan. His older sister was working as a staff nurse, his other sister had just graduated from university, and his younger brother was taking a gap year working in Cambridge. Apart from teenage acne, Tom was a fit and healthy young man, who rarely saw us in the health centre.

He presented on a Saturday morning in May with four days of headache and two days of diplopia on the left lateral gaze. Neurological examination was normal, with no abnormal eye signs. Privately wondering if this could be migrainous or the first presentation of MS, I phoned the duty neurologist who suggested he came up that morning. He was seen and sent home with a working diagnosis of migraine, and the advice to come back if his symptoms did not settle. The headache became more severe, and he started to vomit, so he was admitted to the neurology ward four days later, where he remained for five weeks, until the diagnosis was finally established.

ALAN

People talk a lot about all the waiting in the NHS. We finally persuaded Tom to go to the emergency surgery on a Saturday morning. He was seen just after 9 a.m., referred here and seen by a neurologist at noon. Our experience was that, when it really mattered, you were there for us. In the subsequent weeks, no stone was left unturned in trying to find out what was wrong with Tom and to treat him in the best possible way.

PIPPA

By the time of readmission, there was evidence of a left sixth nerve palsy, which progressed over the following weeks to complete left third, fourth and sixth cranial nerve palsies. Initial CT and MRI scans of the head, carotid angiogram and CSF were all reported as normal. His persistent vomiting proved difficult to control and resulted in him remaining an inpatient for some weeks during the period of investigation. Tom himself pointed out to a doctor a lump under his arm. This was biopsied. As several weeks had passed, the MRI of his head was repeated and this time showed a tiny lesion in the cavernous sinus. The histology revealed metastatic melanoma and a referral to oncology was made.

ALAN

One downside of Tom's time in hospital was the constant struggle to control his symptoms of severe headache and vomiting,
followed by dehydration. We told different doctors again and
again about his vomiting reaction (which he'd had since having
salmonella as a child) and that it was hopeless trying to treat
him with oral anti-emetics and painkillers, but time after time,
he was treated with oral drugs and ended up, after several distressing hours, back on a drip. It's amazing how difficult it was
to communicate that message effectively!

ANNIE

After the diagnosis Tom asked me to inform Stephen, our GP,
who immediately arranged to visit us and to go and see Tom
in hospital. He conveyed a belief that it should be possible to
control Tom's symptoms so he could come home.

Although Tom, and all of us, really wanted him to be at
home, Tom had already chosen to stay in hospital, at least for
the duration of the radiotherapy. There had been one failed and
distressing attempt to treat Tom from home followed by readmission through A & E. He didn't want to risk the pain and
sickness returning, away from the relatively swift relief available
in hospital.

Choice is politically correct these days, but Tom's choice was
based on his difficult experience to date and he, and we, needed
support and assurance to see that it really was worth trying
again with a palliative care regime in place. Stephen listened
to us and encouraged us to believe that the vomiting and pain
could be controlled at home. Within a short time of coming
home, Tom's symptoms were under reasonable control, with
non-oral alternatives at the ready.

It was a success! I won't pretend these times were easy, but we
were able to be ourselves in our own place and the change in

Tom's demeanour was huge! Dying in your own home is something most people want to be able to do. We are really grateful that it was made possible for Tom.

ALAN

I suppose there is no easy way to break bad news. I think we were part of that popular perception that 'they can do such a lot these days with chemo- and radiotherapy'. Like a lot of people, we'd been on the internet, made our own diagnosis and thought about the possible treatments. I remember sitting in the side ward with Tom, Annie and his sisters, listening to the doctor telling us that he had malignant melanoma. Isn't that just skin cancer? Can't they treat it with laser surgery? So it was a truly terrible shock to discover that here was a cancer that was already inside him, and couldn't be touched by any known chemotherapy agent. I wrote a poem about breaking bad news. The original is quite a bit longer, but I think you'll get the gist.

I remember exactly what the doctor said to us.
Blah, blah, blah, blah, blah, blah,
Blah, blah, blah, blah, blah, blah,

Blah, blah, blah, blah, incurable,
Blah, blah, blah, blah, blah, blah.

Yes, I remember every single word.

ANNIE

Actually, despite the terrible shock, we were deeply grateful, over the weeks, for what I would call the 'compassionate honesty' of all the doctors. You were not cruel or unkind, but did not offer us any false hopes. In doing so you helped us, and Tom, to do something really vital – to live each day as fully as we could and to prepare ourselves for his death.

PIPPA

We have made progress in improving treatments for a variety of forms of cancer, but despite this, many patients remain incurable. Oncological treatments sometimes cure, more often offer life extension while, hopefully, maintaining quality of life. Initial breaking of the news of cancer is often undertaken my non-oncologists; this in itself can be devastating. However, the will to survive is immense and oncologists have the difficult task of explaining the realistic expectations of treatment, while trying to leave each individual with an element of hope for their future. In the case of metastatic melanoma, no treatment has yet been shown to impact on survival. We offer most patients treatment within the context of clinical trials of new therapies of unknown benefit. The median age of melanoma patients is in the order of 40 years: it is heartbreaking for patients, their families, and also for the doctors and nurses involved in their care.

STEPHEN

It was invaluable to speak to Pippa before I visited Tom and the family at home. I anticipated discussions around treatment options, and needed up-to-date expert advice. It was particularly important for me to know that while chemotherapy was an option if Tom wanted that, no curative treatment was available, nor any to prolong survival. There was a real partnership between Pippa and myself, with speedy communication by letter, fax and telephone. In a recent study that I have undertaken with Cambridgeshire GPs, it was clear that local GPs greatly appreciate a call from the medical team when a major new diagnosis has been made such as cancer, or a patient has died, and that most of these calls take less than five minutes. Perhaps worth taking up as a Trust policy?

ANNIE

Tom did not find it easy to talk about his situation. So it was really important that he always had time alone with Stephen, as indeed he had with his doctors in hospital. His adult dignity was maintained. I could see how easy it would have been for me, as his mother, to revert to a habit of care more appropriate to an infant, as I watched him go through loss upon loss.

ALAN

And Stephen even spent some time with Tom's mates, helping them to know what to expect, how they could support Tom and what it might mean for themselves. As a result they were able to stick with Tom right through his illness and even came to sit with his body after he'd died – not easy for four awkward 21-year-olds!

ANNIE

Tom remained hopeful for life, but it wasn't long before it became evident that he was facing his death. It was a harsh time, but in the final weeks he was able to live each day at a time, making the most of the times he felt well enough to participate in the life of the household.

ALAN

There were many different medical faces over those months. Our GP, Pippa and her oncology team, neurologists, surgeons, radiologists, receptionists, community nurses, pain control specialists, physiotherapist and a Marie Curie nurse, and a host of others behind the scenes whom we never met. However, we did not experience Tom's care as fragmented. There was continuity of familiar faces and a sense of a multidisciplinary partnership – communicating with each other and with us, all with Tom's best interests at heart.

STEPHEN

Palliative care at home is very much a partnership with the family and lay carers. For Tom, his sister Liz was key, the person he talked to most, and as a nurse even giving PRN IM injections as I had written up. The mates were an important part of his life, and were utterly at a loss to know how to cope with a dying friend, as are most 21-year-olds. With Tom's consent, I met with them on a few occasions, updating them on what was happening, and making some suggestions on introducing some normality and fun into his life. The other key partners were of course the district nurse team, who visited in hospital and made a point of getting to know him and the family early on, so that they were familiar faces when more hands-on nursing care was needed.

ANNIE

Tom was kept supplied with the drugs he needed. There always seemed to be something for the next phase. He was helped to understand the drugs and was able to control his own medication right up to the last couple of days of his life.

ALAN

Helping Tom to make informed choices for himself was one of the most valuable things you did for us. At least he felt somewhat in control, rather than simply being the object of attention, an interesting case at the mercy of others. It did occasionally even have its funny side, like when Tom went to the loo late one night and dropped his syringe driver down the toilet. Thankfully, lo and behold, the emergency services burst into action and within a few hours he had two new syringe drivers! 24-hour care at its best. You really ought to save yourselves some hassle and make them waterproof!

ANNIE

I found it horrifying to see all the drugs stacking up at home. I hated it, but paradoxically I also valued it. It helped me to experience that my instinct to fight for Tom's life wasn't helping him and that collaborating was the best I could do to ease his passage.

ALAN

We were aware, from an early stage, that Tom's case was unusual and interesting from a medical perspective. It didn't happen often, but there were glimpses, occasionally, of a look which said: 'Gosh, what an unusual presentation. How interesting!' And language. All of us in the family were exposed to a vocabulary which was new to us. Words, which mean one thing to you, may mean something quite different to your patients. This poem is called 'Seedlings'.

Tiny seedlings.
So small you can't even see them.
Floating around in a rich, nourishing soup.
Looking for somewhere to land.
A tasty morsel
of nerve
of brain
of armpit
of vocal chord
of liver.

Swimming around.
Eating their fill.
Gorging.
Growing fat.

Eating my beloved son,
Alive.

ANNIE

What for you is familiar technical vocabulary may be slicing into our souls, stirring up all sorts of pain in those you're talking to. You can't avoid it but be aware it may be happening.

PIPPA

Doctors are human beings: we don't always get it right, but we need to be ourselves. We need to be able to say and do the things that come naturally to us, but not be tempted to be defensive and hide behind technobabble: think what it would be like to be on the receiving end of some of the conversations we have; 'cancer progression', 'new growth', 'seedlings', 'harvesting' . . . positive words in everyday use associated with a very different picture in oncology. Be honest, always tell the truth with compassion, reach out and make physical contact, don't be afraid to cry with your patient. Our errors are easily forgiven by patients and families who sense that we really care.

ALAN

Those of us in the family living together with Tom – our task was to do our utmost for Tom, while bearing our own terrible pain at the same time.

ANNIE

As we were different among ourselves, so others will be different from us. There is no typical son-dying-of-malignant-melanoma family. We really appreciated the sense that our strengths were recognized and encouraged and we were shored up in our weaknesses.

STEPHEN

Tom stayed at home from August to his death in October. The week before he died he was still managing to get out of the house. When the end came, it was mercifully swift: he became confused and needed a catheter and syringe driver with diamorphine, midazolam and levomepromazine. As he slipped into a coma, his family sat with him. They were all there when he died.

ALAN

I shall be forever grateful that all of us – Annie and I and his two sisters and brother – were able to be with Tom, in those last days and hours, until he died, in his own bed, at home.

But then, it all suddenly went – the drugs, the special mattress, the syringe driver, the doctors and nurses, our family. Suddenly we are abandoned. Alone.

ANNIE

After Tom's death: the grieving. The harshest time of our lives. Having been so involved in Tom's care up to that point, however – having been able to share those last days and hours with him, having been able to care for his body after death – made grieving less complicated. I believe this to have been one major protective factor in preventing long-term consequences like depression, marriage breakdown, alcoholism, sickness and absenteeism and a long list of secondary miseries, which people who've lost children are so vulnerable to – and which represent a considerable cost to society, not least the NHS!

PIPPA

As an oncologist, I offer the treatments available, while walking with my patient and his family on a final journey, letting go of human life: that's an important part of my job, to help address death and the dying process itself. At some point, I too have to let go of him and his family, handing over to Stephen and his community team, and I also will grieve at the news of life ending, yet with some sense of satisfaction in the hope that my limited contribution made a difference of some kind.

STEPHEN

Looking after Tom was emotionally the hardest task I have had since I qualified, if also deeply rewarding. The family took me inside their circle of love and care, and his death was a real bereavement to me. My district nurse colleagues and I found his funeral an important opportunity to say goodbye.

ALAN

Another major protective factor was the invitation to receive counselling at the Arthur Rank Hospice. A referral had been made to the hospice earlier in Tom's illness, but we did not take that up at the time. Now, after Tom's death, support was offered to us and also to our kids in Nottingham (though they didn't use it). Annie and I both had our own individual support, but this was the only thing we were able to do together, and it was of huge value to us in beginning to knit our lives back together.

ANNIE

When we talked over the preparation for today, someone said: 'We could spend a whole day on this!' So much more we could say, but our time is limited so I will end by saying that all five of us in the family who survived Tom, all of us can remember him with love and pride. Let us be under no illusion. Tom's illness and untimely death were truly terrible, but all of us have been able to make major new steps forward in our lives.

ALAN

It seems like a strange thing to say, but I am quite convinced death is not the worst thing that can happen to you. After all, it happens to the best of us! But how we can support each other in our dying – that is really important – and something for which we will for ever be deeply grateful. Thank you all very much indeed.

Notes

Dedication

1 David Whyte, 'The Well of Grief', from *River Flow: New and selected poems* (Langley, WA: Many Rivers Press, 2012).

4 Loss

1 Genesis 21.16.

5 Bottom line — 1

1 T. S. Eliot, 'Four Quartets', from *Collected Poems* (London: Faber and Faber, 1963).
2 See especially Primo Levi, *If This is a Man* (London: Abacus, 1987).
3 1 Corinthians 13.8, 'Love never fails', NIV; 'Love never ends', NRSV.
4 Romans 8.38–39.
5 Song of Solomon 8.6–7, author's own translation.

6 Visit

1 Philip Larkin, 'An Arundel Tomb', from *Collected Poems* (London: Faber and Faber, 1990).
2 Baroness Sheila Hollins, *Desert Island Discs*, 2012.

7 Help

1 Job 2.10, NRSV, adapted.
2 Mark 14.32–42.
3 Isaiah 53.
4 Michael Mayne, *The Enduring Melody* (London: Darton, Longman & Todd, 2005).

9 End

1 John 12.1–8.
2 Luke 24.

10 Farewell

1 TV series starring Rik Mayall and Adrian Edmondson. Someone who knows them gets them to send Tom a signed photo of themselves in *Bottom*. They write on it: 'Get well, you bastard.' Tom loves it.

2 © Ateliers et Presses de Taizé. Reprinted with permission.

11 KBO

1 Michael Leunig, *A Common Prayer Collection* (North Blackburn, Australia: Dove Collins, 1993).

2 Charles Dickens, *Great Expectations* (London: Penguin Classics, 1994).

3 Annie Hargrave, unpublished poem.

12 Back to work

1 Primo Levi, *If This is a Man* (London: Abacus, 1987).

13 Moving on

1 Genesis 32.22–32.

2 The Collect for the Fourth Sunday before Lent.

14 New life

1 Dr Evelyn Sharp, consultant psychiatrist, Oxleas NHS Foundation Trust and InterHealth Worldwide.

2 Psalm 139.14.

3 Pat Barker, *Regeneration* (London: Penguin, 1992).

4 Ewan MacColl, from *Black and Whiter* (London: Cooking Vinyl, 1990).

15 Leaving

1 Alan Boyd, unpublished poem.

16 The Grand Round

1 For full text, see Appendix.

17 Bottom line — 2

1 Philip Larkin, 'Churchgoing', from *The Less Deceived* (Hessle, East Yorkshire: Marvell Press, 1977).
2 George Herbert, 'Bitter Sweet', from *The English Poems of George Herbert* (Littlehampton Book Services, Worthing/Everyman, 1974).
3 Hebrews 12.1–2.
4 John 20.24–28.
5 Nicholas Wolterstorff, *Lament for a Son* (London: SPCK, 1997).
6 Mara means 'bitter'. See Ruth 1.20.
7 Lo-ruhamah means 'not pitied'. See Hosea 1.6.
8 Annie Hargrave, unpublished poem.
9 Jeanette Winterson, *Why Be Happy When You Could Be Normal?* (London: Vintage, 2012).

18 Blessed

1 C. S. Lewis, *A Grief Observed* (London: Faber and Faber, 1966).
2 Nicholas Wolterstorff, *Lament for a Son* (London: SPCK, 1997).
3 R. S. Thomas, 'Folk Tale', from *Collected Poems* (London: Phoenix, 1993).
4 The Sacrament of the Present Moment is a Christian concept first expounded by Jean-Pierre de Caussade, similar to mindfulness in Buddhism.
5 William Shakespeare, *Hamlet*, Act 1, Scene 3.
6 For the importance of 'stability', see Alan Hargrave, *Living Well* (London: SPCK, 2010) and the Rule of Benedict. Benedictine vows include a vow of 'stability', which in practice means remaining in the same community for life.
7 Viktor Frankl, *Man's Search for Meaning* (London: Rider, 1959).
8 George Herbert, 'Gratefulnesse', from *The English Poems of George Herbert* (Littlehampton Book Services, Worthing/Everyman, 1974).
9 Edward the Confessor, as he was dying, was reported to have said, 'Weep not, I shall not die. And as I leave the land of the dying I trust to see the blessings of the Lord in the land of the living.'